PRAISE FOR JOEY CLIFT

"Joey Clift weaves humor, heart, and a palpable Indigenous spirit. He is an artist to watch!"

— ***Mark Ruffalo***
Actor

"Wow. I feel like I want to watch everything Joey's ever done. [Gone Native is] really fun and straight to the point."

— ***Sequoia Carrillo***
NPR

"[Clift] offers cheeky solutions to fans who may miss performing the Tomahawk chop or wearing redface."

— ***Kylie Cheung***
Salon

"Joey Clift has not only dedicated his life to doing some of the most insane, imaginative bits and concepts onstage . . . but as a proud member of the Cowlitz tribe, Clift has pushed for visibility and representation for Native and Indigenous talent in comedy and elsewhere."

— ***Jake Kroeger***
The Comedy Bureau

PRAISE FOR *WE'VE BEEN HERE THE WHOLE TIME!*

"*We've Been Here the Whole Time!* is a refreshing, satirical take on Native history that doesn't shy away from the absurdities and contradictions, offering a laugh-out-loud perspective that's as enlightening as it is entertaining."

— ***Dr. Anton Treuer*** *(Ojibwe)*
Author of Everything You Wanted to Know about Indians but Were Afraid to Ask *and* Where Wolves Don't Die

"Sharply written, frequently hilarious, and educational as hell!"

— ***Aaron Reynolds***
New York Times *bestselling author of* Effin' Birds

"Clift's wry and amusing new book delights and enlightens at the same time. Dispelling stereotypes and extinguishing myths, *We've Been Here the Whole Time!* might very well turn an ignoramus into an intellectual."

— ***Kliph Nesteroff***
Author of The Comedians *and* We Had a Little Real Estate Problem

"I've worked with Joey for a number of years, and this book is a perfect combination of his humor and history. Give it a go!"

— ***Charlie Berens***
Comedian, New York Times *bestselling author of* The Midwest Survival Guide

"A throwback to the funny history books I cherished so dearly growing up in the '90s, like *Horrible Histories* meets the modern bite of *The Onion*. A hilarious, accessible gateway to incredible facts and history most of us missed in school."

— ***Chelsea Rebecca***
Producer & host of the Dead Meat Podcast

"Joey Clift is not just one of the funniest writers in Indian Country—he really knows his stuff. This book is a win for Natives everywhere. If it had been around back in the day, I wouldn't have answered so many stupid questions in school . . . from my teachers."

— ***Azie Dungey*** *(Pamunkey)*
TV writer of Unbreakable Kimmy Schmidt and Rutherford Falls

“When I teach Indigenous history, I always search for creative materials that allow me to teach the history and contemporary reality of Indigenous peoples in the United States. And while there is a plethora of materials, hardly any of them bring a fresh, comedic approach to so serious a topic. In this book, Cowlitz author Joey Clift does that. Using humor and what I would describe as NDN wit, Clift allows us to see three-dimensional perspectives of Indigenous history, culture, and people, as well as critiques of settler colonialism in the funniest way possible.

“You will learn about everything from the athletic prowess of Jim Thorpe to critiques of land acknowledgements and colonial uses of Spirit Animals and who ain’t invited to the powwow. This book is perfect to gift to your disgruntled relative, your Indigenous auntie, or your teacher who claims they don’t know enough about Indigenous history and culture to teach it. If you’re an educator, this book will soon be an essential part of your teaching materials—and you will laugh. Out. Loud. Clift has written a book that represents some of the best work in Indian Country. A must-read!”

— ***Dr. Kyle T. Mays***
(Black & Saginaw Chippewa)
Author of An Afro-Indigenous History of the United States

WE'VE BEEN HERE THE WHOLE TIME!

WE'VE BEEN HERE THE WHOLE TIME!

A Not So Sacred Guide to All Things Native America

JOEY CLIFT

Illustrations by Julie Fiveash

Andrews McMeel
PUBLISHING®

WE'VE BEEN HERE THE WHOLE TIME: A NOT SO SACRED GUIDE TO ALL THINGS NATIVE AMERICA

The authorized representative in the EEA is Simon and Schuster Netherlands BV, Herculesplein 96 3584 AA Utrecht, Netherlands. (info@simonandschuster.nl)

Andrews McMeel Publishing
a division of Andrews McMeel Universal
1130 Walnut Street, Kansas City, Missouri 64106

www.andrewsmcmeel.com

26 27 28 29 30 TEN 10 9 8 7 6 5 4 3 2 1

ISBN: 979-8-8816-1088-3

Library of Congress Control Number: 2026939305

Editor: Amanda Meadows
Designers: Julie Barnes and Gina Martin
Production Editor: Dayten Rose
Production Manager: Jeff Preuss

MIX
Paper | Supporting responsible forestry
FSC® C016973
FSC www.fsc.org

This book is dedicated to the first Native who was ever asked a weird question by a colonizer. I don't know what the question was, but I'm sure it made them kind of roll their eyes and take a deep breath before answering.

You are all of us.

CONTENTS

SECTION THREE: HONORS INDIAN TACOS 73

FOREWORD

If you've picked up this book, I'm going to assume one of two things about you.

Either you're Native and someone told you, "Oh my god, you have to read this, it'll make you feel seen," which, depending on your tribe, means you were immediately suspicious and flipped to the back to check who wasn't invited to the powwow.

Or you're a well-meaning non-Native person who has realized, sometime in the last few years, that everything you were taught about us was a little light on detail. Maybe you're trying to be better. Maybe you're trying not to embarrass yourself. Maybe you already have and you're hoping this book will teach you how to never do that again. *Brave of you*, honestly.

Either way, you bought this book with real money, which earns you at least two stars in whatever afterlife you end up in.

What you're holding is not a history textbook. It's not a sociology treatise. And it's not one of those books that promises to "explain Indigenous peoples in ten easy steps" but was clearly written by someone whose closest interaction with us was watching *Smoke Signals* once.

This book is a *full-body welcome* into Joey Clift's particular brand of clarity through chaos. He has a way of sneaking the truth up on you halfway through a joke, tapping you on the shoulder, and saying, "Hey, that thing you thought you knew? Let's fix that." He weaves humor, irritation, and joy into something sharp enough to puncture centuries of confusion, yet soft enough to share with your aunt who insists her 23andMe results should guarantee her magical casino money.

Joey and I come from different corners of the Indigenous creative world. He leans comedy and animation; I lean horror and sci-fi literature. But our jobs are, at their core, the same. We use story to make sense of the ongoing oddity of being Native in a country that still acts surprised we exist.

That's the thread running under this whole book. Beneath the diagrams, lists, and flowcharts, Joey is doing what Indigenous storytellers have always done: offering context, correction, and a mirror. Not the sad museum kind but the funhouse type that shows all the distortions people have projected onto us. You're about to hit jokes that seem harmless until you realize they're doing real historical work. Punchlines, charts, and side-eye commentary so clean you won't notice how much you learned until the chapter is over. It's a rare skill to teach and entertain at the same time, and Joey makes it feel natural.

If you're non-Native, don't worry. He's not here to shame you. He's here to *save you from yourself*, which is a different service entirely. He's filling in the gaps your football-coach-turned-history-teacher left behind. The ones you didn't know were there. The ones you've stepped into before without realizing, like potholes on a rez road.

And this book isn't a lecture. *It's a ride.*

What I love most is that this book arrives at exactly the right moment. More people now realize Native stories exist beyond buffalo-shaped worksheets and tragic museum plaques. Native writers, actors, athletes, and animators are everywhere. Not as mascots or metaphors but as full, contradictory, hilarious humans. There's a shift happening, not because the world suddenly became more welcoming but because Native creators keep pushing their stories into rooms that once pretended not to see us.

And here comes Joey Clift, handing readers a survival guide disguised as a comedy manual. *Not survival for us. Survival for you.* For anyone who has hesitated before asking a Native coworker a question. For anyone who wonders why "my great-grandma was a 'Cherokee princess'" makes Natives within fifty feet develop a sudden migraine. For anyone who wants to do better but doesn't know where to start.

This book *is* your better.

If you're Native, this book is a treat. You'll read chapters and think, *Finally someone said it.* You'll feel that spark of recognition our communities pass down like recipes, beadwork patterns, or that way we all stare at white folks who claim *we're all indigenous to somewhere*.

The humor here comes from familiarity, from family, from the exhaustion and joy of being asked the same questions for five hundred years and finding new ways to answer without losing your mind. But it also comes from generosity. Joey knows laughter opens doors faster than scolding. He knows humor makes the truth easier to carry and harder to forget.

And that's the magic of his work. He writes for both audiences at once without losing either. Plenty of Native creators aim inward, speaking directly to community. Plenty aim outward, translating us for a wider world. Writing for both without flattening us or softening the blows takes skill, patience, and the *particular* kind of humor that grows in places where the absurd and sacred live side by side.

If you're Native, this book will feel like your auntie pulling up a chair and saying, "I'm telling you this because I care, but also because you're *being a shitass*."

If you're non-Native, this book will feel like someone tossed you a rope right before you said something you'd regret for the rest of your life.

Either way, hold on.

You're in good hands. Joey Clift is the kind of storyteller who can make you laugh at something you didn't know was funny and then make you care about something you didn't know was *missing*.

So go ahead. Turn the page. Learn something. Get roasted a little. Laugh a lot. And when you're done, carry the jokes with you and let the truth settle in where it needs to.

And if this book teaches you even one thing that keeps you from asking a Native person something wild in the future, congratulations. You've already gotten your money's worth.

— ***Shane Hawk*** *(Cheyenne-Arapaho)*
ShaneHawk.com

Pick up
Never Whistle at Night: An Indigenous Dark Fiction Anthology
wherever books are sold!

INTRODUCTION

Or, why me and your teachers have beef!

Before picking up this book, chances are the only time you ever learned about Native American peoples was in elementary school while your teacher showed you how to make hand turkeys the week of Thanksgiving. Though I'm sure your teacher was fantastic and your hand turkey was to *die* for, that five-minute lesson probably wasn't enough to cover every detail about the Indigenous peoples who lived on this continent before Columbus sailed the ocean blue.

I know they didn't teach you much because I, as a Native American person living in the twenty-first century, have been asked a lot of wild questions by college-educated adults who really should have known better. Questions like, "Were you born in a teepee?," "Does your reservation have electricity?," and "Do you have magic powers?" The answers to those questions are "No," "Yes," and "No, but one of my uncles does. (ayyy)"

The recent research project "Reclaiming Native Truth" discovered that a big reason for those questions is that 87% of United States schools don't teach Native American history past 1900. For most people, after the Wounded Knee Massacre, they think Native people just kind of disappeared, I guess?

If your history or social studies teachers didn't teach you about American Indians, then the responsibility now rests on my sage Indigenous shoulders. I'm Joey. I'm an enrolled member of the Cowlitz Indian Tribe, and I grew up on the Tulalip Reservation. It's great to meet you!

To help you navigate the complexities and sacred/sacrit wisdom of Indian Country, this book is broken into four sections.

Remedial Leathers and Feathers covers the super basics, like how we can't all transform into animals like Natives in movies from the 2000s. Well, Taylor Lautner can, but he's not actually Native, so that's just a *him* thing.

Basic Indigen-ometry goes a little deeper, explaining Indigenous-themed sports mascots and how long Lewis and Clark would have survived the Oregon Trail without their guide Sacagawea. Spoiler: Not long!

Honors Indian Tacos explores more nuanced topics like Pretendians and why my tribe's casino rocks. Seriously, it's called Ilani, and it's about a twenty-minute drive north of Portland, Oregon. It has not one but two cafés and a burger restaurant owned by Paul Stanley and Gene Simmons of KISS! Are Paul Stanley and Gene Simmons chefs? No!

AP Tribal Council Member dives into the big issues, like the Land Back movement and how the Founding Fathers stole the United States' system of government from Indigenous peoples. I mean, they stole a lot of stuff from Indigenous peoples, but I digress.

This book is for Natives to laugh along with and relate to and for non-Natives to hopefully learn something that their schools never bothered to teach them. You'll read biographies of Indigenous heroes like Joe Medicine Crow and Deb Haaland, see helpful flowcharts like "When is it okay to touch a Native person's hair?," learn about cool, historic Indigenous events like the Occupation of Alcatraz in the 1960s, and read a whole list of people who aren't invited to the powwow. If you're wondering if Christopher Columbus is on that list, let's just say he's first. What can I say, Native people can hold a grudge!

If you want to be helpful and maybe a little passive-aggressive, this book would make a great gift for your well-meaning coworker who keeps calling meetings powwows, or your "spiritual" friend who insists her grandmother is a Cherokee princess, or your new-age aunt who thinks she might be Indigenous because an eagle looked at her once.

I hope that in reading this book, you laugh, learn, and then laugh again nervously because you read something that you're embarrassed that you didn't know and you just realized that you might be the butt of the joke (it's okay). This book won't get you an Indian name, but if it leads to you asking Native folks fewer weird questions, I'll consider it a win.

As a reward for getting this far, here's a hand turkey.

SECTION ONE

REMEDIAL LEATHERS AND FEATHERS

Put away that loincloth and grab a Jim Thorpe jersey. It's time to get remedial!

WAIT, AREN'T NATIVE AMERICAN PEOPLE EXTINCT?

No! It's weird that you felt the need to ask this question!

We're still here, and one of us even wrote this book.

A second one is standing behind you right now!

Just kidding. Or am I?

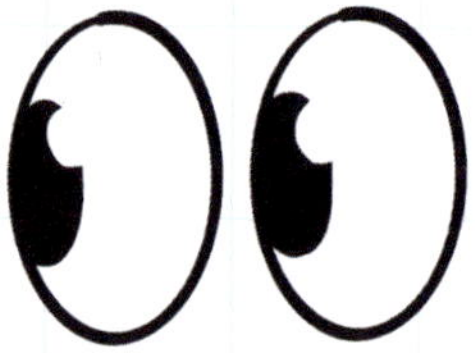

MATH LESSON

Native people by the numbers

Throw away your calculators because I'm giving you numbers in the most sacred form of all: charts and graphs!

How Many Native People Are There, in Millions?

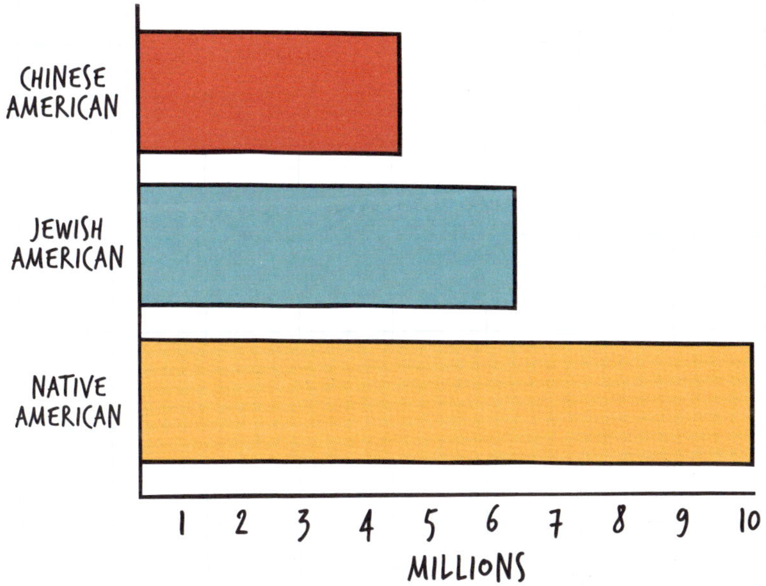

According to the 2020 United States census, there are around ten million Native folks living in the USA. We're similar in population size to the Jewish American and Chinese American populations. Not only are we not extinct—we're not rare either—but we're all special in our own way!

How Many Tribes Are There in the USA?

There are over 570 federally recognized tribes and hundreds more that are state-recognized. Globally, there are at least five thousand Indigenous nations. Wow!

How Many Reservations Are There?

There are over three hundred reservations in the United States. Some tribes don't have their own reservation, and others share reservations. Most Natives don't live on reservations; we live in cities and on your pull-out couch if you'll let us (just wash the comforter please, we're not trying to get bed bugs).

What Is the Biggest Tribe?

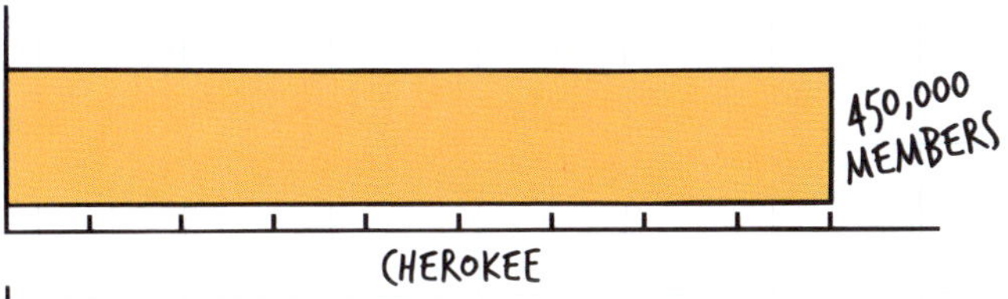

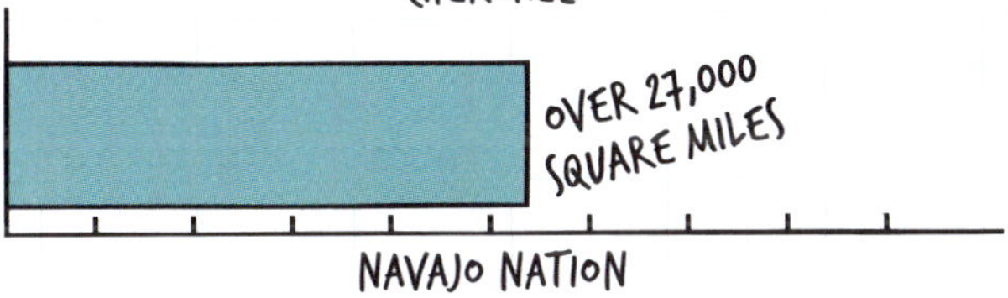

The Navajo Nation has the largest reservation in the US. It covers parts of New Mexico, Arizona, and Utah. It's about the size of West Virginia. The Cherokee have the most members and, when it comes to population, about as many people as the state of Wyoming!

What Is the Smallest Tribe?

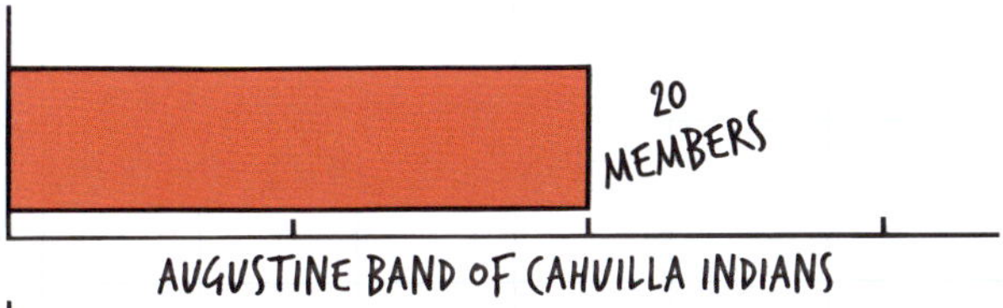

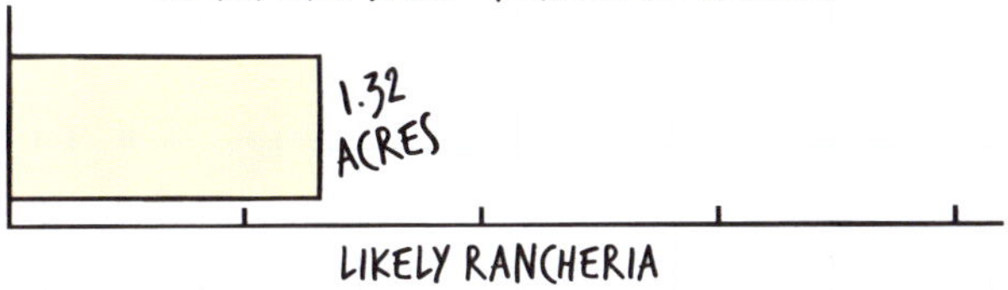

Some tribes are tiny. The Augustine Band of Cahuilla Indians has only twenty members. One of the Pit River Tribe's reservations is a little over an acre and is mainly used as a tribal cemetery. Before you get too sad, the Pit River people have around two thousand living members, own many businesses, have other reservations in the American Southwest, and are doing great!

What Is the Best Tribe?

My tribe. The Cowlitz. We rock! Did I tell you about our casino, Ilani, which is a short drive north of Portland, Oregon?!

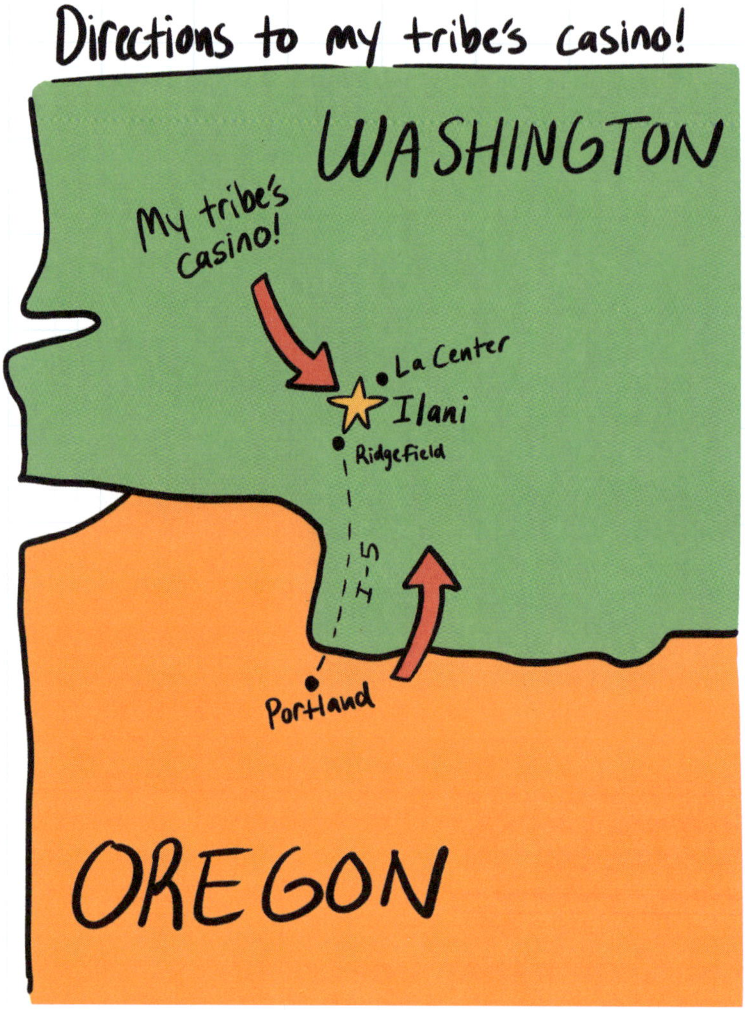

WHAT THE HECK DO WE CALL YOU?

A deep dive!

From "American Indian" to "Native American," non-Natives often wonder about the proper way to address North American Indigenous people. Here are some common terms and how I personally feel about them!

INDIAN: When Columbus landed in the Americas, he thought he was in India, so he referred to all of the local Indigenous people as "Indians," and the name stuck, despite the people he met not being from, or even living close to, India. Weird!

The term's use continued, making its way into official United States government documents. The people within the federal government who handle Indigenous issues are called the "Bureau of Indian Affairs"; on our treaties with the United States, our tribes are referred to as "Indian Tribes"; and the Declaration of Independence refers to us as "merciless Indian Savages" (yikes!).

Though Native people have different views on being referred to as an "Indian," it is a term you'll often hear on reservations. Like many of these terms, it's okay for members of a culture to refer to each other as that. Does it feel a little strange when "non-Indians" use that term? Yes!

AMERICAN INDIAN: See Indian. At some point, "American" was added to "Indian" to at least differentiate "Indians" from "people from India." It's been five hundred years, and Christopher Columbus is still making life confusing and difficult for people all across the planet. Thanks, Chris!

INJUN: Gross. Why would you say this?

REDSKIN: This is a dictionary-defined racial slur. We prefer to be called "Commanders" now.

ESKIMO: This is also a racial slur. If you say it to, or around, Alaska Native folks or friends of Alaska Natives, the chances of you getting punched in the face is not low!

> Author Note: I just want to highlight again, the above two words are slurs. Though it's important to include them here, uncensored for context, all other uses of those words in this book will only be direct quotes (and it only happens like once per word) because I want this to be an enjoyable read for everyone and I don't want to get beat up by anyone's cousin. Okay, now that that's out of the way . . .

NDN: Shorthand for "Indian," because why use six letters when three will do fine?

INDIGENOUS: Though this term is technically accurate and few people will take offense to being called it, it's a bit too broad to specifically refer to Indigenous people from North America. There are Indigenous peoples all across the globe, and Native American or American Indian people are a tiny subset of that community.

FIRST NATIONS: This is the blanket term for the Indigenous peoples of Canada, and I'm so jealous because come on, it sounds so rad.

NATIVE AMERICAN: This term became popular during the civil rights era of the 1960s, around the same time "African American" entered into use. Though this term at least makes it harder to confuse us with people born on the Indian subcontinent, it makes it *easier* to confuse us with people born in America.

Imagine, as a Native American (Indigenous) person, having to explain to someone who is not Indigenous that just because they were born in Nashville, that doesn't mean they are a "Native American from Nashville." This kind of confusion happens too often and is exhausting.

Additionally, many Native folks don't like this term because it defines us by our connection to the United States of America, which many North American Indigenous folks feel a *little* conflicted about because of the whole "centuries of attempted genocide by the government and also we were here before America" thing.

NATIVE: This term is closer to what people who are Indigenous to the North American continent refer to each other as on a regular basis. It's easy, convenient, and cool to say! Though the same confusion exists when using this term around non-Natives as with the term "Native American." Being "Native" because you are Indigenous and being "native" because you were born, raised, and still live in Nashville are not the same thing. One is to claim association with an ethnic group/tribal nation, while the other is just a shorthand way of saying you were born someplace. And what's my problem with Nashville, you ask? Andrew Jackson is buried there, and as you will learn later, he sucks!

REFERRING TO A GROUP OF INDIGENOUS PEOPLES BY THEIR TRIBE: This is the most accurate and safe way to refer to any group of Indigenous peoples. For example, I am not an "Indian," I am "Cowlitz," meaning that I am an enrolled member of the Cowlitz Indian Tribe.

Granted, there are hundreds of unique tribes in the United States and many more Indigenous peoples around the world, and it would be a lot to expect any one person to have all of those memorized, but if you could try to memorize some of them, it would be pretty cool.

If that sounds like too much work, don't blame me. Blame Christopher Columbus.

SORRY, WE AREN'T WEREWOLVES

(But *Twilight* book series author Stephenie Meyer is!)

In her fictional *Twilight* book series, author Stephenie Meyer claims that members of the very real Quileute Tribe of Washington State are werewolves. Though the books came out decades ago, it's still causing problems for the Quileute!

Twilight fans have desecrated Quileute burial sites, stolen Quileute cultural items, and even called the Quileute tribal offices to ask, "Can y'all turn into wolves?" This for real happens and is truly insane. Meyer hasn't apologized for this and made these claims with zero facts or research. Some people think she was being thoughtless when she wrote that stuff, but I think she might be covering for something.

After my own extensive detective work, here are a few reasons I think *Twilight* author Stephenie Meyer is actually a werewolf:

- Stephenie Meyer was born in Hartford, Connecticut. Since the 1920s, Hartford has had its own professional hockey team called the Hartford Wolf Pack. Coincidence? I think not!
- There aren't any widely available photos of Stephenie Meyer in front of a full moon in her human form. Shocking!
- When Stephenie Meyer visited the *Twilight* film set, the set allegedly smelled kind of like wet dog, but there weren't any dogs on set that day!
- Stephenie Meyer didn't consult with the Quileute Tribe at all or receive any permission from them when claiming that the Quileute are werewolves in her book series. No human is dumb enough to do that, so the only other option is that Meyer has the brain of a wolf!

- One time when I visited a wolf sanctuary, I said Stephenie Meyer's name out loud and all of the wolves at the sanctuary perked up a little bit.
- According to a friend of mine, Stephenie Meyer eats with her hands and never uses silverware. Guess what kind of metal werewolves hate? *Right?!*
- If you take the third word of every page of *New Moon* and put them all together, it gives you a long nonsense sentence—the same kind of sentence a wolf would write!
- Meyer has brown hair, and take a wild guess what color fur some of the wolves in the *Twilight* movies have? Brown. I rest my case.

AN EASY ACRONYM TO REMEMBER ALL FIVE-HUNDRED-PLUS FEDERALLY RECOGNIZED TRIBES IN THE UNITED STATES

There are over five hundred federally recognized tribes in the United States. Each tribe is its own sovereign nation with its own unique cultures and customs.

It can be hard to remember the names of so many tribal nations, so I've constructed this simple-to-remember acronym to help! Ready? Let's go!

A-A-A-A-A-A-A-A-A-B-B-B-B-B-B-B-B-B-B-B-B-B-C-C-
-C-C-C-C-C-C-C-C-C-C-C-C-C-C-C-C-C-C-C-C-C-C-
C-C-C-C-C-C-C-C-C-C-C-C-C-C-C-C-C-C-C-C-C-D-D-
-D-D-E-E-E-E-E-E-E-E-F-F-F-F-F-F-F-F-F-F-G-G-G-G-G-
H-H-H-H-H-H-H-H-H-H-I-I-I-I-I-J-J-J-J-J-K-K-K-K-K-K-
K-K-K-K-K-K-K-K-K-L-L-L-L-L-L-L-L-L-L-L-L-L-L-L-L-L-L-M-
-M-M-M-M-M-M-M-M-M-M-M-M-M-M-M-M-M-M-M-M-
M-M-N-N-N-N-N-N-N-N-N-N-N-O-O-O-O-O-O-O-O-P-P-
P-P-P-P-P-P-P-P-P-P-P-P-P-P-P-P-P-P-P-P-P-P-P-P-P-P-
P-P-P-P-P-P-P-P-P-P-P-P-P-P-Q-Q-Q-Q-Q-R-R-R-R-R-R-
R-R-R-R-R-S-S-S-S-S-S-S-S-S-S-S-S-S-S-S-S-S-S-S-S-S-
S-S-S-S-S-S-S-S-S-S-S-S-S-S-S-S-S-S-S-S-S-S-S-S-S-S-
S-T-T-T-T-T-T-T-T-T-T-T-T-T-T-T-T-T-T-T-T-T-U-U-U-U-U-
-U-U-U-W-W-W-W-W-W-W-W-W-W-Y-Y-Y-Y-Y-Y-Y-Y-Y-Z

That was just the three hundred or so federally recognized tribes that make up the lower forty-eight states. Now here's an acronym to remember all of the tribes based out of Alaska!

A-A-A-A-A-A-A-A-A-A-A-B-B-C-C-C-C-C-C-C-C-C-C-C-C-C-D-E-E-E-E-G-G-H-H-H-H-H-H-I-I-I-I-K-K-K-K-K-K-K-K-K-K-K-L-L-M-M-M-M-M-N-O-O-O-O-O-O-O-P-P-P-P-P-P-P-P-Q-Q-R-S-S-S-S-S-S-S-S-S-S-T-T-T-T-T-T-T-U-U-V-V-V-V-V-V-V-V-V-V-V-V-V-V-V-V-V-V-V-V-V-W-Y-Y

Now, that was for the tribes that are federally recognized. Some tribes, for reasons such as colonization, treaties, and differing federal recognition criteria, are only recognized by state governments. Here are some simple acronyms you can use to remember many of the state-recognized tribes!

Alabama: **C-C-C-E-M-M-P-S-U**

Connecticut: **E-T-S**

Delaware: **L-N**

Georgia: **C-G-L**

Louisiana: **A-B-C-C-F-G-I-L-N-P-U**

Maryland: **P-P**

Massachusetts: **N**

New Jersey: **N-R-T**

New York: **T-T-U**

North Carolina: **C-H-M-O-S-W**

South Carolina: **B-E-P-P-S-T-W**

Vermont: **E-K-M-N**

Virginia: **C-C-E-M-M-N-N-P-P-R-U**

Are these acronyms long and crazy? Sure, but in your US History class, you probably had to learn the names of all fifty states and their capitals. If your teacher made you memorize that Jefferson City is the capital of Missouri (so confusing!), it's only fair that you learn a few local tribe names too. If the names of all five-hundred-plus federally recognized and all one-hundred-plus state-recognized tribes in the USA are too much to memorize, all you have to do is say these acronyms and smile at your status as an educated ally!

THESE PEOPLE AREN'T INVITED TO THE POWWOW #1

Christopher Columbus

Powwows. The centerpiece of Indian Country. Part cultural event, part dance party, part illegal fireworks convention. Natives and non-Natives of all types are invited to celebrate. Except for these jerks. And for our first entry, we're starting with the biggest jerk of all, Christopher Columbus.

Born in Genoa, Italy, in 1451, Columbus is most famous for crossing the Atlantic Ocean in 1492. Despite sucking at everything he tried, Columbus received his own holiday, celebrated somewhere around October 12, the anniversary of the day he "discovered" the Americas. That sounds impressive, for sure, but if you look into it at all, Columbus bumbled his way through life like a genocidal Mr. Bean.

The reason for Columbus's first voyage was to find a faster trade route to India. He was hired by Spanish royalty to map that route, and not only did he land in the Americas instead of India, he never even visited India in his whole life! He had one job, to visit India, and he couldn't even do that!

When he accidentally landed in the Bahamas, he was so convinced that he'd landed in India that he called the Indigenous peoples of the Bahamas "Indians." The name stuck, and now whenever I try to find restaurants that sell Indian tacos, I get a million tikka masala recipes instead. Now, I LOVE tikka masala, but it's not the same thing!

Instead of thinking the Earth was round, which was an established fact for thousands of years even in the 1400s, Columbus stupidly thought the Earth was shaped like a pear. This is real and so dumb. It was because he was awful at math and navigation, and due to his poor calculations, that he thought the Earth was way smaller than it is.

This is fun to laugh at, but it also put his crew of around a hundred men on his first voyage at real risk. Since he'd prepared for a shorter trip based on his straight-up wrong math, his men would have run out of supplies and eaten each other LONG before reaching India. Columbus sucking at his job wasn't a secret; his crew even attempted a mutiny against him two days before they landed in the Americas because they were concerned his bad leadership would get them killed.

And Columbus being a terrible leader wasn't a one-time thing. As a reward for "discovering" America, he was made governor of modern-day Haiti and the Dominican Republic. He was so bad at governing that he was arrested for incompetence. Imagine being so bad at something that your boss throws you in jail (how embarrassing). Then there's this insane and real excerpt from the journal of his earliest voyage describing when he saw a manatee for the first time.

> *On the previous day, when the Admiral went to the Rio del Oro, he saw three mermaids, which rose well out of the sea; but they are not so beautiful as they are painted, though to some extent they have the form of a human face.*
>
> –Christopher Columbus
> Wednesday, 9th of January 1493

First question, did Columbus think a manatee was a mermaid? One hundred percent yes.

And now a second, more pressing question. Did Columbus and his men have sex with a manatee because they thought it was a mermaid?! The answer is "maybe" leaning toward "oh hell yeah they did."

All of this makes Columbus look like an idiot, but that's not even the dark stuff. He and his men were true tyrants. When they first met the peaceful Arawak, Taino, and Lucayan people, they repaid the local Indigenous peoples' kindness by raping, kidnapping, and selling many of them into slavery. Assuming the Caribbean was filled with gold, Columbus forced the local Indigenous people to labor in mines until they died of exhaustion, beheading all who refused to work.

Within two years, an estimated 250,000 Haitians died or were murdered because of Columbus's actions and orders. There are even reports of Columbus and his men butchering Indigenous men, women, and even babies and using their meat to feed Columbus's own dogs.

Though colonization in a broad sense can be blamed for a lot of Indigenous trauma, the negative effects that Columbus specifically had on the people of the Caribbean and South America are still felt over half a millennium later. To claim that this man deserves any honor whitewashes a list of monstrous crimes committed by him and his men that, if written out, would stretch across the ocean.

There's also the whole "discovery" thing. How can you discover a place when people already live there? It'd be like me saying I discovered Spain because I accidentally got off the train in Barcelona on my way from London to Rome. Columbus Day only became a federal holiday in 1971. It's not even as old as *Diamonds Are Forever*, the seventh James Bond movie, so it's not like celebrating him is some long, time-honored tradition. Also, why doesn't James Bond have a holiday? He's way cooler than crusty Chris.

Christopher Columbus is definitely not invited to the powwow, but if after all of this you still want to celebrate Columbus Day, I ask that you move it from October 12, the day he landed in the Bahamas, to January 9, the day he and his men probably had sex with a manatee. That way, we're celebrating him for what he actually was: a big, weird dummy.

FLOWCHART: EVERY TIME IT'S APPROPRIATE TO TOUCH A NATIVE AMERICAN PERSON'S HAIR

If there's one thing non-Natives love doing, it's touching a Native person's long, flowing hair. If you see a Native person with a mane of hair so lush that it would make even Saulteaux First Nation actor Adam Beach jealous and you desperately want to run your fingers through it, here's an easy flowchart to tell you when that's okay!

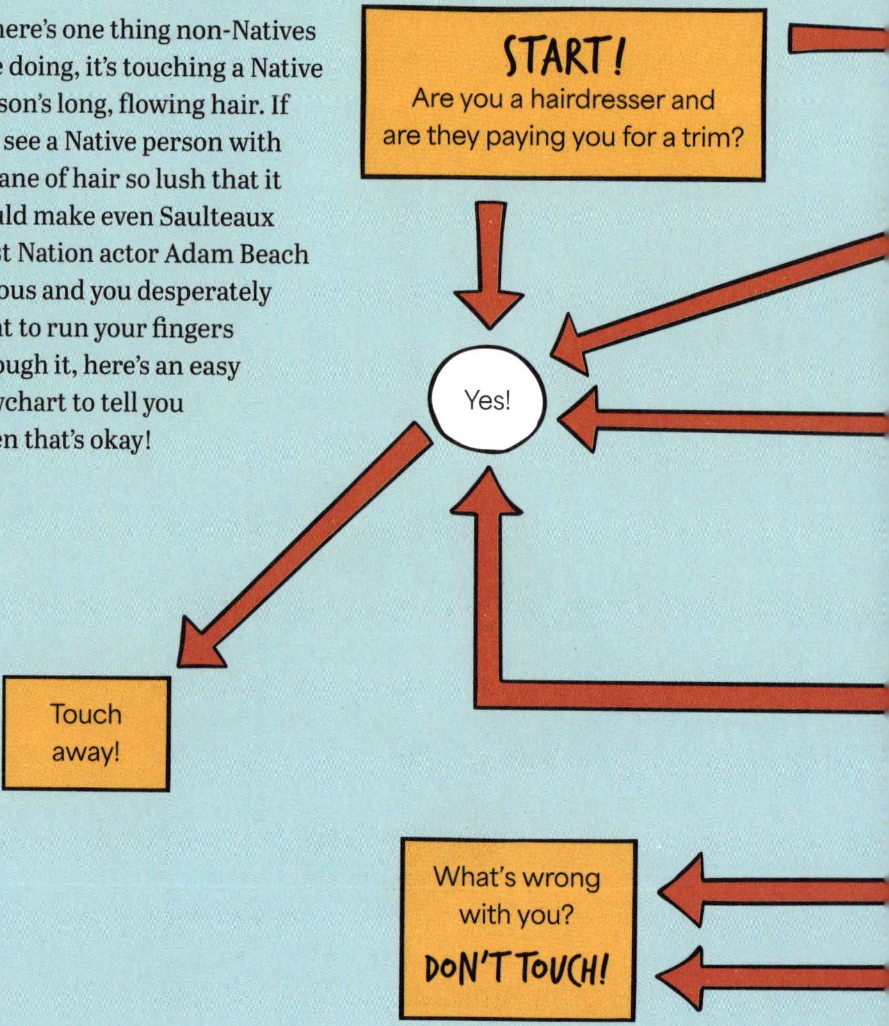

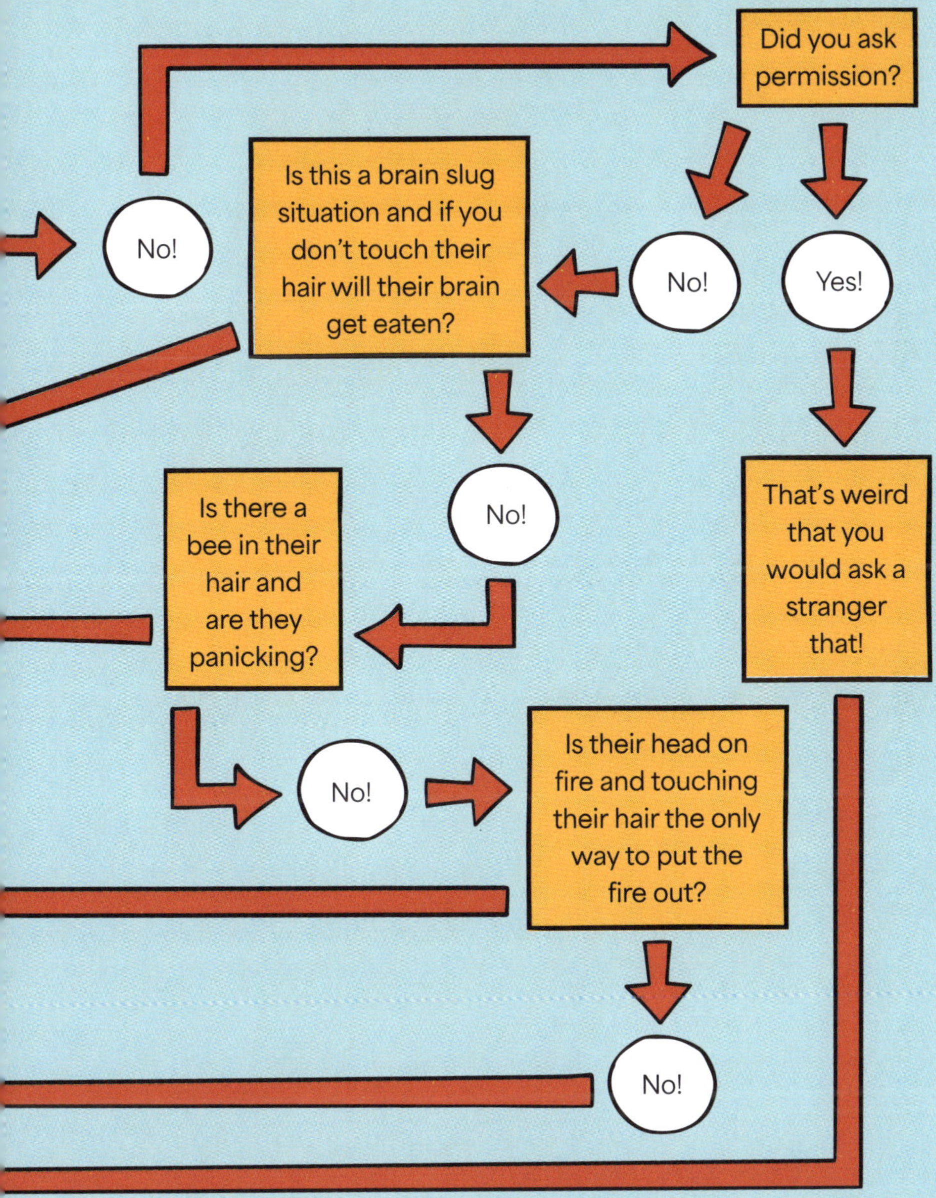
No!
Did you ask permission?
No!
Yes!
Is this a brain slug situation and if you don't touch their hair will their brain get eaten?
That's weird that you would ask a stranger that!
No!
Is there a bee in their hair and are they panicking?
No!
Is their head on fire and touching their hair the only way to put the fire out?
No!

COOL MOMENTS IN INDIGENOUS HISTORY #1

Cahokia

Oftentimes, when non-Natives are taught about Indigenous peoples from precolonization, we're described as an unorganized collection of small tribes who didn't do anything good or noteworthy. First off, how dare you? Second off, that's so far from the truth that it might as well be in outer space.

One of the largest organized settlements in the world in approximately 1100 AD was an Indigenous settlement a few miles from what is now St. Louis, Missouri. It was called Cahokia, and it was awesome!

Though no records have been found of the exact tribal makeup of Cahokia, it was located where the Mississippi River connects with other major rivers, so experts believe it was a hub used by different tribes to trade things like copper and shark teeth, which is so metal that I'm headbanging just thinking about it.

Cahokia wasn't only used as a place to trade pre-film Jaws memorabilia. It was also a huge city! Even the present remains of Cahokia stretch six square miles, making up over a hundred buildings. At its biggest, Cahokia is estimated to have had a population of around twenty thousand people, which was even bigger than London at the time. Suck it, 1100s AD monarch Henry I of England!

HENRY.I.

It's hard to keep twenty thousand people fed, unless you're the geniuses running Cahokia a thousand years ago! It's believed that Cahokia had the means to store grain and other foods, as well as a complex irrigation system used to raise enough crops to supply the entire city. They even had organized sports and a large calendar made out of timbers called "Woodhenge" that helped them track the seasons! Anyone using Stonehenge to claim European seniority should shush right about now, because Natives had literally the same technology but made theirs with classy wood instead of dusty rocks.

Personally, I think Cahokia is so cool because it underlines that Native people were doing great stuff in the Americas before Columbus decided to drop a fresh steaming Chris all over the Americas. We were as advanced as and, in some ways, even more advanced than our European counterparts at the time. We excelled in areas like agriculture, where we innovated a "companion planting" system still in use today (shout-out to the three sisters: corn, beans, and squash!). We were also more sanitary and all around healthier. While British nobility spent their days hobbled by gout, Natives of the Americas played early versions of lacrosse. Our multi-story pueblos and big structures, like the pyramids of South America, predate many European megastructures. The astronomical knowledge of many tribes lapped those of European explorers.

Though archeologists aren't sure what happened to Cahokia, Natives built something big, noteworthy, and 100% their own thing without the help of even a single European colonist. Archeologists also found the remains of caffeinated drinks all over Cahokia's mounds, so not only was Cahokia larger than London, they also had tea like half a millennium before them too. God, the United Kingdom are such copycats.

A LIST OF THINGS YOU CAN ASK NATIVE PEOPLE ABOUT THAT AREN'T THANKSGIVING

"How do you feel about Thanksgiving?" is a question non-Natives LOVE asking us because it's a holiday that's kind of about celebrating our genocide maybe? It's a loaded question for a lot of Native people, so to make things easier for you, here is a list of things you can ask Natives about that aren't Thanksgiving!

1. Cats
2. Dogs
3. Video games
4. Cherokee film actor Wes Studi
5. Desserts (not pumpkin pie)
6. Health insurance
7. The iconic filmography of Cherokee film actor Wes Studi
8. Professional wrestling
9. The ongoing controversy of pineapple on pizza
10. Toyota Corolla hatchbacks
11. Cherokee film actor Wes Studi's relationship status
12. The weather
13. Can one talk about the weather without talking about climate change? (This is rhetorical.)
14. If Wes Studi's relationship status is "single," would you introduce him to my mom? She's very lonely.
15. Mashed potatoes (but be careful! Mashed potatoes could be a gateway to asking about Thanksgiving!)
16. Would Ryan Gosling be a good Batman?
17. Would Austin Butler be a good Batman?

18. Would Wes Studi be a good Batman? (And by Batman, I mean "father-in-law." That casting has my blessing!)

19. Sports (but if you're asking about sports so you can then ask, "How do you feel about the Kansas City Chiefs?," that's exactly as weird as asking about Thanksgiving!)
20. AI (as long as AI doesn't stand for "Amazing! I can finally ask you all of my Thanksgiving questions!")

If after reading this list, you still want to ask Native people about Thanksgiving, don't! Just google it. The first Thanksgiving was hundreds of years ago and we're tired.

YOU'RE WELCOME! #1

Space exploration

Native people are responsible for a ton of great stuff, but we rarely get any credit for all we do. I know, right?! Not only is the United States government taking credit for the land they Manifest Destiny-ed from us, they're also taking credit for our ideas! It's not too late to let us say "you're welcome," starting off with the contributions Native folks made in the exploration of the final frontier: space!

Space isn't a foreign concept to Indigenous people. Native folks had stories and legends about the stars for generations. The Diné of the southwestern United States told tales of Coyote, a trickster who used a ladder to climb up to the stars to create the constellations as a prank (ayy). The Northern Athabaskan people of Alaska used star mapping for everything from navigation to forecasting the weather, and it's not just them. Indigenous nations from the Māori people of New Zealand to the Maya of Central America all had their own unique forms of "Indigenous astronomy."

And this isn't "ancient sacred wisdom." Native people make huge contributions to space exploration to this day! One of the most influential people in the history of space travel is Cherokee Nation citizen Mary Golda Ross.

Ross, born in 1908, was a genius-level mechanical engineer and extremely proud of her Cherokee culture. Even a summary of her accomplishments would take a whole 'nother book, but here are some highlights:

- Ross was the first woman mechanical engineer hired by influential aerospace manufacturer Lockheed Corporation.
- She was a founding engineer of "Skunk Works," which was a section of Lockheed dedicated to making top-secret aircraft that helped win the Cold War, and she was the only woman on the team.
- She made massive contributions to the Agena rocket project, which was a significant part of the United States' first manned missions to space.
- She literally cowrote NASA's Planetary Flight Handbook, a guide for space flight to Mars and Venus, which is still in use!

Keep in mind, Ross's career spanned from the 1940s to the 1970s. Most of her calculations were done with a pencil and slide rule. Since much of her work was part of top-secret programs, a lot of it is still classified, so we don't even know all of the amazing stuff she did. What we do know is she's a Native aerospace Matriarch with a capital M!

Since Ross retired in the 1970s, she spent her later years pushing for women and Native folks to pursue careers in engineering. Today, dozens of badass Natives work in the aerospace industry, including folks like Diné engineer Aaron Yazzie, who helps create drill bits used by rovers on Mars, and Mississippi Choctaw tribal member Powtawche N. Valerino, a navigation engineer who helps direct unmanned spacecraft to our literal blazing hot sun.

There's also Chickasaw tribal member John Herrington and Round Valley Indian Tribal member Nicole Aunapu Mann, the first Native man and woman in space.

Of course, space travel takes a huge team, and I'm not claiming that Native people are solely responsible for all of humanity's journeys to the stars, but we played a bigger part than most people know and most colonizers give us credit for. For that, I say:

TWO HUNDRED PERCENT OF NATIVES AGREE WITH ME

Why most polls of Indian Country are total bullshit

Telling Native people they're wrong is a common hobby for many non-Natives. It's like a delicious drink to them, and they're always thirsty. One of the ways they do that is through polling, where a handful of Natives are asked about a specific issue and non-Natives will use the results about that poll as the ultimate "I'm right, you're wrong" defense.

drink it up,
colonizers

The thing about those polls is they're usually conducted by people who don't know anything about Indian Country. For example, *The Washington Post* conducted this poll in 2016:

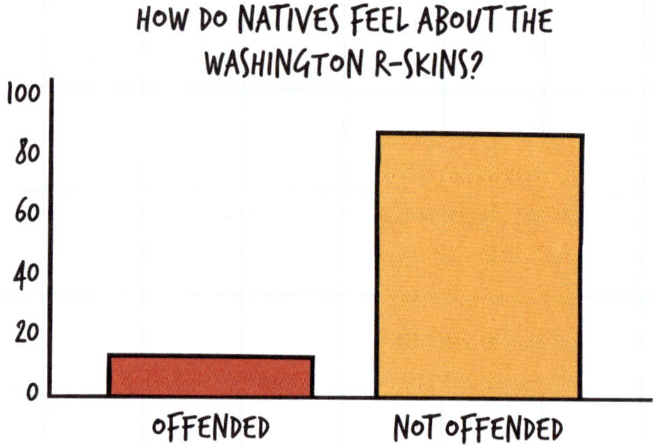

If you've ever had a conversation with someone who is defending Native sports mascots, they'll often bring up this poll, saying "90% of Natives don't mind the Washington R-Skins" as CONCLUSIVE PROOF that using Native people as mascots is completely okay.

The thing is this poll is bad data. The *Post* only asked five hundred "self-identified" Native people. Who are those people? What tribe are they from? How many of them aren't actually Native, but they "feel Native" because they love Disney's *Pocahontas*? We don't know because *The Washington Post* didn't ask.

More recently, a 2024 poll from Edison Research showed that, by percentage, Natives voted for Donald Trump more than any other group. This made national news with the claim that 65% of Natives voted for him compared to 58% of white voters. What most outlets didn't report is that they only polled 229 *self-identified* Native people, and <u>none</u> of these polls were conducted on reservations.

Additionally, Native people are often combined with other, unrelated groups, like a 2020s CNN election poll that had categories for white, Black, Latino, Asian, and "Something Else."

Not only is this data useless, but erasing us from polls is another way to erase the problems and issues Indian Country faces every day; it's also terrible journalism. I'm not saying that polling Indian Country is impossible. I'm saying that there are a lot of us, from hundreds of unique tribal nations and all kinds of socioeconomic backgrounds. We aren't a monolith; we're all different people from different places and with different opinions. You're not going to get useful data about all of us from groups inexperienced in Indian Country, interviewing a couple hundred "self-identified" Native people.

So, in short, most polls of Indian Country aren't worth the paper they're printed on, with one exception. This conclusive poll.

What percentage of Natives think Ilani is the best casino?

WHEN IS IT OKAY TO CALL SOMEONE AN "INDIAN GIVER"?

Oh god, gross. Why the hell would you ask this? How about never?!

INDIGENOUS EXCELLENCE #1

Jim Thorpe

"You, sir, are the greatest athlete in the world."

–King Gustav V of Sweden

"I don't usually listen to the King of Sweden, but that guy has a point!"

–Me

Indigenous people don't have to prove that we're excellent to deserve basic human rights (we should get those anyway because, come on), but for fun, here are a few Indigenous folks who kicked a ton of butt at the top of their fields, starting with badass Native super athlete Jim Thorpe.

Jim Thorpe of the Sac and Fox Nation of Oklahoma was basically Indigenous Superman. Born in 1887, Thorpe was a top-level athlete in every sport he played, including professional basketball, baseball, and football.

He was so respected for his time playing football that he was elected as the first president of a tiny little mom-and pop-organization called the National Football League, which nowadays runs a teensy-weensy yearly cultural juggernaut called the Super Bowl.

That's insanely impressive, and that's not even his coolest accomplishment within football! That belongs to the time he, playing for the Carlisle Indian School, stomped the hell out of the US Military Academy at West Point, beating them 27–6. It's poetic that a bunch of Indians beat the best the United States military had to offer a couple decades after the Indian Removal Act emboldened that same military to forcibly remove Native folks from their homelands. What's even more poetic is that Thorpe was playing across the field from West Point's star halfback and future president Dwight D. Eisenhower.

There's speculation that Eisenhower sustained a career-ending knee injury while trying to tackle Thorpe, but what isn't speculated is that Eisenhower complained about how insane of a player Thorpe was like fifty years later in a speech closing out his second presidential term. Dude helped win World War II, served two terms as president, and was absolutely HAUNTED by how bad Thorpe beat him!

Thorpe wasn't only a god at football, he was also an Olympic-level athlete, scoring two gold medals in the 1912 games in Sweden. Thorpe took home the gold in the pentathlon and the decathlon.

Reading this, you're probably thinking to yourself, "Wow! This Jim Thorpe fella sounds like the best athlete ever!" But it gets even more crazy!

The night before the games, someone stole Thorpe's shoes. The pentathlon and decathlon involve a LOT of running, and instead of forfeiting because he literally didn't have shoes to run in, Thorpe went to his nearest garbage can, fished out two old sneakers, and when he noticed that one of the shoes was a few sizes too big, he put on an extra pair of socks and won two gold medals anyway! And those wins weren't close. He dominated so hard in the decathlon that the record he established wasn't beaten until 1948, almost forty years later!

Though most of Thorpe's major accomplishments were in the 1910s and 1920s, he was so impressive as an athlete that in 2000, in an ABC Sports poll, he was named the "Greatest Athlete of the 20th Century." People used to say Michael Jordan was so good at basketball that his name became synonymous with "the best." Well, Thorpe was like if Michael Jordan wasn't just the best at basketball, but he was the best at all other sports too!

And sports weren't the only thing Thorpe was great at; he was also a prolific actor who used his fame to advocate for other Natives in entertainment when no one else would. He was so respected that when he passed away, a town in Pennsylvania was renamed "Jim Thorpe" so the residents could borrow a little of his shine.

I could write a million words about how cool Jim Thorpe was. Instead, I'll leave you with President Eisenhower's bitter complaint about him in that speech given, once again, nearly **fifty years** after losing to Thorpe!

There are some people who are supremely endowed. My memory goes back to Jim Thorpe. He never practiced in his life, and he could do anything better than any other football player I ever saw. If we have any of those geniuses around here, they don't have to work—but all the rest of us do.

—President Dwight D. Eisenhower

SECTION TWO

BASIC INDIGEN-OMETRY

Now that you've got the remedial stuff about Native people out of the way, here's an ever so slightly higher bar you can step over!

SIXTEEN WAYS TO HONOR NATIVE PEOPLE THAT AREN'T NAMING YOUR SPORTS TEAM AFTER US

From the Kansas City Chiefs to the Atlanta Braves, there are around two thousand "Native themed" sports teams in the United States.

Some people believe these teams should change their names because there is compelling research connecting Native sports mascots to low self-esteem and high suicide rates among Native kids. Other people think we should keep them because they're "honoring" us, I guess?

Whichever side you're on, I've come up with easy ways to honor us that don't involve sports at all!

1. Watch the hit television show *Reservation Dogs* and give it a perfect score on IMDB!
2. Go to a tribe's powwow, buy an Indian taco, and then tell the person that made it, "Hey, that Indian taco was delicious!"
3. Listen to the song "Where Is the Love?" by Black Eyed Peas, but just the Taboo verse.

4. Learn the names of five Native people. Bonus points if they're still alive!
5. Go to a bookstore, find all of the copies of *The Only Good Indians* by Stephen Graham Jones, and put them on the "Employees' Picks" shelf even if you don't work there.
6. If you own a sports team or company that uses a Native as the logo, donate some of your profits to actual Native people maybe!
7. Watch the 2016 superhero movie *Suicide Squad* and cry extra hard when Adam Beach's character dies. It happens early in the movie so get your tissues ready!
8. Get a trophy made that says "The Best" on it and then go to a Native arts market and give it to the oldest Native person there.
9. If you're in a crowded area, mutter under your breath, "Lily Gladstone should have won that Oscar . . ."
10. If you're thinking about doing the Tomahawk Chop or wearing redface at a sporting event, don't!
11. Look at a picture of trailblazing Native politician and activist Deb Haaland and smile and nod at her knowingly.

12. If you tell a Native person "I'm honoring you" after you do something weird, and the Native person says, "That actually doesn't honor me," shut up and take the L!
13. If you disagree with some Native-related issue or platform, don't track down a tiny group of Native people who agree with you and then use that group as an echo chamber to justify your beliefs. That has nothing to do with honoring us or not honoring us. It just happens a lot and is weird and dumb!
14. Go to Mt. Rushmore and give it a thumbs-down!
15. Go to the grave of the guy who built Mt. Rushmore and give it a thumbs-up! (The thumbs-up is not celebrating his art. It's celebrating that he's not alive!)
16. Gamble at a tribal casino, and if you win any money, give it back!

Author Note: You don't HAVE to do this at my tribe's casino, Ilani, but if you did, I wouldn't hate it!

LAND ACKNOWLEDGMENTS AND YOU

How to acknowledge the land without looking like a total dingus!

A lot of people think of "land acknowledgments" as a phrase liberals throw around on the internet, or the kind of thing you've heard an usher say as they're dripping with nervous "I hope I don't mess this up" sweat right before a movie. It's not only done for woke points: There are good reasons to do it too! Simply put, a land acknowledgment is a short statement at the start of a gathering to thank the original caretakers of the land you are currently on. Native folks have done these for years and years, and non-Native folks recently started getting in on the action!

Now, as someone who's performed many land acknowledgments, I'm going to give you a little constructive criticism. It's great when non-Natives perform them, but when they do it, it pretty much always makes my skin crawl a little bit. Here are some tips to help you acknowledge the land without looking like a doofus.

Actually do a land acknowledgment! This one feels obvious, but the first step to doing a good land acknowledgment is to actually do one. Don't say, "Hey, we should do a land acknowledgment" and then forget about it. It takes like twenty seconds, come on.

Figure out which tribe or tribes' land you're acknowledging! Sorry about being such a stickler about this, but if you plan on doing a land acknowledgment, maybe figure out which peoples you actually plan on acknowledging? If you don't know this information off the top of your head, then you're in luck. There are a ton of great resources, like native-land.ca, which can help you figure that out in seconds.

Not naming a specific tribe in your land acknowledgement would be like me thanking "Europeans" for inventing spaghetti, which would be silly.

Pronounce the name of the tribe correctly. I know, I know. I'm setting a high standard here, but when you're acknowledging a tribe, it would be base-level respectful if you tried to pronounce their name kind of right. You'd be surprised how many people get this one wrong. If you don't know how to pronounce a tribe's name correctly, might I suggest Google?

Don't ask the ONE Native person you know to do the land acknowledgment for you! Look, I'm sorry this whole thing has so many steps, but this one is maybe the most important. Having a Native person do a land acknowledgment doesn't give you extra points you can redeem in Native Heaven. If they're from the tribe whose land you're acknowledging, you're basically asking them to thank themselves, which, if so, you're welcome?

Also, don't ask the only Native person you know but haven't talked to since high school to do the land acknowledgment. If you slide into the DMs of a Native you met at a party like ten years ago to say, "You up and also you willing to acknowledge the land?" they're probably going to be at least a little annoyed, and their annoyance will be more than a little justified!

If you do a land acknowledgment over Zoom, which Indigenous peoples are you acknowledging? And is their aboriginal territory Reddit? If you're not doing a land acknowledgment in a physical location, maybe ask everyone to drop the names of the tribes whose territory they're on in the chat? Otherwise, I'll assume you're acknowledging the original stewards of the internet: AOL Chatroom users!

Prepare your land acknowledgment in advance. Usually "We should do a land acknowledgment!" is an idea people have right before their gathering starts, and it's usually followed by a panicked thirty seconds where everyone is trying to figure out how to do one. If that's you right now, here's an easy-to-follow script!

> *We acknowledge that the* (Name of Tribe/s) *people are the traditional land caretakers of* (City you're in) *where* (this gathering) *is located. The* (Name of Tribe/s) *people took care of this land for thousands of years, they're still here and they rock. Also, a special shout-out to Joey Clift for writing this land acknowledgment. Buy his book, please!*

That last part is the most important part, so don't forget it! (ayyy)

Maybe do a little more than just a land acknowledgment. I'm being selfish, I know, but instead of telling Native people, "Hey, thanks for taking care of this land," have you thought of doing something useful?

Land acknowledgments are nice, but what would be even nicer is if you gave us our land back. Or, if you don't have land you can give us, do a minute of research to see if your local tribe or tribes have cultural centers looking for volunteers or any tribally owned businesses you could spend money at. Unfortunately, our landlords don't accept land acknowledgments as a rent payment, but if they did that would be real kind of them. Plus, every dollar you spend at a Native-owned business lets Jim Thorpe buy even more meat pies in Native Heaven!

LEWIS AND CLARK: A CASE STUDY

How long would Lewis and Clark have survived their expedition without Sacagawea?

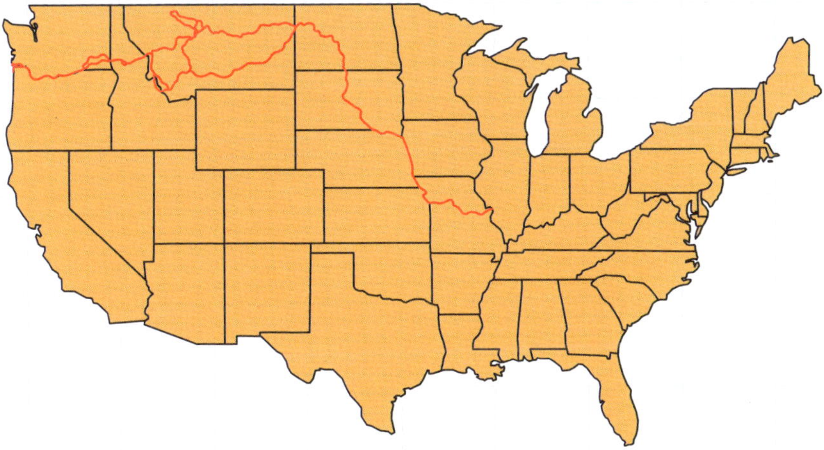

Lewis and Clark Expedition

The Lewis and Clark Expedition was an eight-thousand-mile-long hike in 1804 where Meriwether Lewis, William Clark, and a team of explorers surveyed a large section of the United States that had recently been bought from France as part of the "Louisiana Purchase."

The expedition started in St. Louis and ended in what is now Oregon. It was a long, grueling, and dangerous trip and is often used as an example of the enduring American spirit. Turn the page to see how long they would have survived without their "Indian guide" Sacagawea!

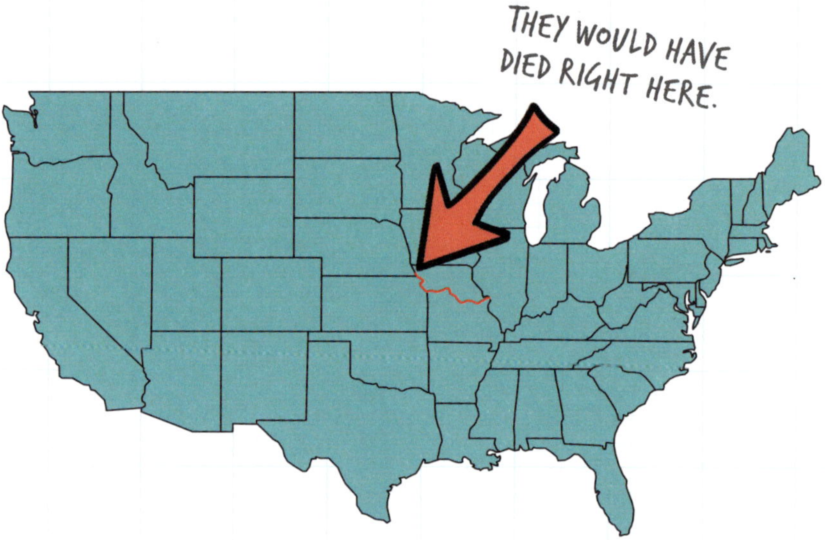

Lewis and Clark Expedition without Sacagawea

Lewis and Clark would have totally died eating poison berries like ten minutes after leaving St. Louis. Not only was Sacagawea key in telling those dorks what berries to eat, she also knew the land and was friends with some of the local tribes. When Lewis and Clark inevitably pissed those tribes off, Sacagawea told the tribal leaders, "I know these guys are dumb, but please don't kill them."

What's especially crazy about this is that during the Corps of Discovery's expedition, Sacagawea was only sixteen! Even the United States government, which RARELY gives credit to Native folks, decided that Sacagawea's swag was too hard to ignore, so they put her on dollar coins starting in 2000. Lewis and Clark are also on commemorative coins, but instead of getting their own individual coins, they had to share one, like total losers.

COOL MOMENTS IN INDIGENOUS HISTORY #2

The Fort Laramie Treaty and how Natives took over Alcatraz

In the late 1800s, the United States government was at war with a ton of tribes across the continent, fighting to steal land from Native folks in the name of colonization. Because Natives are great warriors (it's a stereotype, but it's a good one, so I'll take it), the USA eventually decided to sign treaties with tribes to end all of these separate wars.

The Fort Laramie Treaty of 1868, between the USA and the Sioux, is one of those treaties, establishing the Great Sioux Reservation of South Dakota. It gave the Sioux a place to live while the USA colonized the rest of Sioux territory.

Of course, the United States, as they're known to do, immediately went back on their deal, but treaty law is a story for another section. The Fort Laramie Treaty contains this excerpt.

> *. . . any male Indians over eighteen years of age, of any band or tribe that is or shall hereafter become a party to this treaty, who now is or who shall hereafter become a resident or occupant of any reservation or territory not included in the tract of country designated and described in this treaty for the permanent home of the Indians, which is not mineral land, nor reserved by the United States for special purposes other than Indian occupation, and who shall have made improvements thereon of the value of two hundred dollars or more, and continuously occupied the same as a homestead for the term of three years, shall be entitled to receive from the United States a patent for one hundred and sixty acres of land including his said improvements . . .*
>
> –Fort Laramie Treaty excerpt

In normal human terms, this means that if a Sioux person starts living on any unclaimed federal land, that person will receive ownership of that land, plus a little extra land if they're feeling spicy.

What exactly is unclaimed federal land? Any land the government deserts, abandons, or just says, "We don't want it anymore!"

So what would happen if the United States government were to abandon a prominent piece of federal land, like, for example, when they closed San Francisco's famous Alcatraz penitentiary in 1963? Well, reader, Natives swooped in and took that thing over.

When news stories broke announcing the decommissioning of Alcatraz, a member of the Rosebud Sioux Tribe living in the Bay Area named Belva Cottier researched the Fort Laramie Treaty and realized that she could legally claim the whole Alcatraz island. She hired a lawyer and, in a baller move, offered to buy the land at forty-seven cents per acre, which was the same amount the US government offered for the Sioux's land nearly a hundred years prior.

After a few years of figuring it out, and after a fire burned down San Francisco's only Indian community center, the local Native community decided to "just do it" like Jordan in a Nike ad and hired a bunch of boats to take them to the island.

For nearly two years, Native activists and students traveled to Alcatraz, building a camp on the island totaling over four hundred people at its peak. In those two years, they set up a daycare, clinic, kitchen, and even their own radio station hosted by Santee Dakota legend John Trudell.

These "Radio Free Alcatraz" broadcasts were listened to daily by over **one hundred thousand** people. This made the United States government furious. The FBI even started a file on John Trudell, writing that he was "extremely eloquent, therefore extremely dangerous," which is a bland, bureaucratic way of saying, "It's scary how much fire he spits!"

Celebrities like Marlon Brando, Jane Fonda, and Jonathan Winters visited Alcatraz to show their support for the Native folks who had taken over the island. Creedence Clearwater Revival even donated over ten thousand dollars to the occupiers, which was used to purchase a boat to ferry activists to and from the island. It was a whole big thing! That means if you've ever listened to CCR's hit song "Have You Ever Seen the Rain?," a percentage of those royalties might have been used to help Native folks fight the government, which is dang radical.

After a nearly two-year siege where the government shut off power and water and did everything they could to keep supplies from getting to the island, the dozen or so remaining Native folks were forcibly removed. But the thing is, the Native folks won!

The occupation led to changes in federal policy through bills like the Indian Self-Determination and Education Assistance Act of 1975, which granted tribes increased autonomy with less federal oversight, and the Blue Lake Act of 1970, which saw the return of forty-eight thousand acres of land to the Taos Pueblo people of New Mexico. Though the occupiers weren't allowed to keep Alcatraz as Sioux property, the occupation convinced the government to give the island to the National Park Service so they could preserve and memorialize what happened there.

If you visit Alcatraz today, you can still see the words "Indians Welcome" painted in huge letters on the side of one of the main buildings.

The actions of the Alcatraz occupiers even inspired other Natives to stand up and make similar claims, like the activists who took over Fort Lawton in Seattle, Washington, in the 1970s. That ended with the government giving those activists dozens of acres of land, which they used to build the Daybreak Star Cultural Center, a gathering place for Native folks and allies in Seattle that is still in use today.

Why there isn't a movie about this stuff starring Lily Gladstone and Wes Studi, I have no idea. I mean, come on. Lily Gladstone as a badass lawyer using the Fort Laramie Treaty to win the deed to Alcatraz and Wes Studi as her uncle who's also an experienced getaway driver? That's a license to print money! And people will love it when, in the third act, there's like ten car chases that end with them jumping a Cadillac over Alcatraz right as Lily Gladstone says an ice-cold catchphrase. It practically writes itself! I mean, just look at this cool movie poster I made!

You can't tell me you wouldn't watch this!

A COMPLETE LIST OF PEOPLE YOU CAN CALL "POCAHONTAS" WITHOUT BEING RACIST

1. The Actual Pocahontas (whose real name wasn't even Pocahontas, it was Matoaka BTW!)

2. Disney's Pocahontas

3. There is no 3, that's the whole list.

THESE PEOPLE AREN'T INVITED TO THE POWWOW #2

Andrew Jackson

Columbus had his powwow rights revoked for being a greedy idiot who maybe had sex with a manatee. Andrew Jackson, on the other hand, made the list for being a murderous psychopath. When I say he was a murderer, I don't mean that by signing the Indian Removal Act of 1830 he caused the tragic deaths of several thousand Native folks (though that is true). I mean he literally murdered a guy and got away with it. His name was Charles Dickinson. Look it up!

Referred to as "The People's President," Jackson was elected largely due to his rags-to-riches story. Raised in poverty in the late 1700s, Jackson eventually rose to be one of the wealthiest people in the country. That sounds admirable unless you ask how he got his money.

Hint: It was buying and selling humans!

When he became United States President in the 1820s, Jackson had enslaved over 150 people, and his cruelty had no limits. One example of his jerk behavior comes from the time he offered a ten-dollar bounty for every one hundred lashes delivered to one of his runaway enslaved people. As president, he fought anti-slavery legislation with the same fierceness he used to fight the guy he murdered. He even referred to anyone against slavery as "monsters." This had to have been one of history's biggest moments of "you're one to talk."

Aside from putting the "pro" in the phrase "professional human trafficker and murderer," Jackson was also obsessed with Native tribal nations. He spent most of his life fighting to forcibly remove Native people from their traditional homelands so the government could steal their territory. He even referred to Native folks as "his red children," which is a weird thing to say all around. I mean, what the hell, Andy?

The Indian Removal Act was basically his sole legislative victory in his eight years as president, and it wasn't even a real victory. The Supreme Court at the time immediately named the forcible relocation of tribes as unconstitutional in the case Cherokee Nation v. Georgia. Good old Murderin' AJ didn't take no for an answer and told state governments to remove Native people anyway.

He accomplished this by forcing different tribes to sign "removal treaties" that gave them reservation land west of the Mississippi, mostly in what is now Oklahoma and parts of Kansas. He also offered supplies, food, and the agreement to help settle the relocated Indigenous peoples in their new territories. If a tribe didn't sign, Jackson told them he would send the Army after them. Around seventy of these treaties were signed.

The thing is, Jackson lied about all of that, and the payments he promised to Native folks were given to shady contractors who stole the money and didn't build anything. Also, instead of going through any proper tribal authorities to make these treaty deals, Jackson found random collections of Native folks and convinced them to sign on behalf of their people. It'd be like if I tried to get ownership over Utah and my legal document only had the signature of some guy I met in a bar in Park City. A lot of Native folks didn't even know they were being relocated until the Army showed up with bayonets, forcing them off their homelands.

Around a dozen tribes, including the Cherokee, Chickasaw, Ho-Chunk, Creek, and Choctaw were affected by the Indian Removal Act, and each tribe had their own tragic relocation events called "the Trails of Tears." Around fifty thousand Native folks were forcibly relocated, and over ten thousand died on the several-thousand-mile journeys to their government-assigned reservations. Nearly two hundred years later, we're still feeling the effects, with many languages lost and generations of Natives living in the painful aftermath, all so some settlers could make a few extra bucks.

As an example for how screwed up all of this was, Adolf Hitler patterned much of his attempted genocide of Jewish people in Europe after Andrew Jackson's policies, going as far as saying the Volga River of Russia would be "our Mississippi."

Though Jackson being a cruel owner of enslaved people and land thief/genocidal freak is all public knowledge, you wouldn't know it visiting Andrew Jackson's Hermitage, his mansion-turned-museum located near Nashville, Tennessee. They instead focus on his family and upbringing. In researching this book, I visited his Hermitage, where I heard from experts and guides about his lifetime of service. In a particularly somber moment, the tour guide showed us the bedroom where former President Jackson died of tuberculosis in 1845.

Signs around the room requested that visitors not take pictures in the bedroom or of the bed where Jackson lived his final moments as a show of respect. I decided to be the bigger man and honor those wishes.

Just kidding. I took a picture of the bed he died in so fast, and you can see it here.

I would like to add one great thing about Jackson. He reportedly cursed so much in life that his pet parrot had to be removed from the funeral for swearing, which is SO funny. President Jackson will never be invited to the powwow, but his potty-mouthed parrot? She's in.

Even my small bird brain is smart enough to know that you're SCUM!
poop
Andrew Jackson

QUIZ: WHICH CHARACTER FROM *THE OFFICE* IS YOUR SPIRIT ANIMAL?

Do you love the classic sitcom *The Office*? In this simple quiz, you'll learn which hilarious Dunder Mifflin employee is your Spirit Animal!

Question 1: Who would you rather have lunch with?

1. Jim
2. Pam
3. Dwight
4. Michael

Question 2: What is your favorite *The Office* quote?

1. That's what she said.
2. I declare bankruptcy!
3. They're the same picture.
4. I am Beyonce, always.

Question 3: If you could hide Dwight's office supplies anywhere, where would you hide them?

1. Jello
2. Schrute Farms
3. The Warehouse
4. Scranton Mall

Question 4: Who was a better manager at Dunder Mifflin?

1. Michael
2. Creed
3. Deangelo
4. Nellie

Question 5: What's your favorite food to eat at work?

1. Chili
2. Tuna
3. Beets
4. Microwave popcarn

Question 6: What is your Dunder Mifflin dream job?

1. Salesman
2. Regional Manager
3. Accountant
4. Warehouse Foreman

Question 7: You're at *The Office* Christmas party. What would you rather be doing?

1. Hanging out with Kelly
2. Pranking Dwight
3. Petting cats with Angela
4. Doing the Scott's Tots dance

Now put down your stapler-filled Jello mold, add up your points, and turn the page to find out which character from *The Office* is your Spirit Animal!

NONE OF THEM!

A quiz isn't how you get a Spirit Animal.
It doesn't work like that!

Receiving a Spirit Animal is a specific and culturally significant event in many Indigenous nations. It's a rite of passage that often involves days of fasting, prayer, and guidance from cultural experts in our communities. Not everyone does it because it's hard to do, but when it happens, it's a cause for celebration. It's like being awarded a fancy medal but in the form of a nice wild creature. Saying that one of the characters from *The Office* is your Spirit Animal devalues that whole important process. It's like saying you've got a Purple Heart when instead of being in the Army, you just bought one from a dusty thrift store.

If you want to say that a fictional character is "my Spirit Animal," maybe instead say, "I like that character!" If you must appropriate a culture while explaining how much you like Chester Cheetah or whatever, might I suggest saying that character is your "patron saint"? The Pope is very busy counting all of the riches the Catholic Church stole from Indigenous peoples, so he won't notice you using their term, I promise.

And if after reading this, you still want to know which character from *The Office* is your Spirit Animal, it's Phyllis. You're welcome!

FLOWCHART: IF YOU OWN A DREAM CATCHER, DO YOU SUCK?

Like totem poles, eagles, and the show *Reservation Dogs*, one of the things people most associate with Natives is the dreamcatcher. Though they were created hundreds of years ago by the Ojibwe (or Lakota, depending on who you ask), they've become a pan-Indian symbol for Native culture and identity. Plus, they look so stylish hanging over a bed.

They're so popular nowadays that a dreamcatcher can be bought at most gas stations or gift shops in North America, and they're produced everywhere from South Dakota to China. But if you own a dreamcatcher, do you suck? Find out in this super simple flowchart.

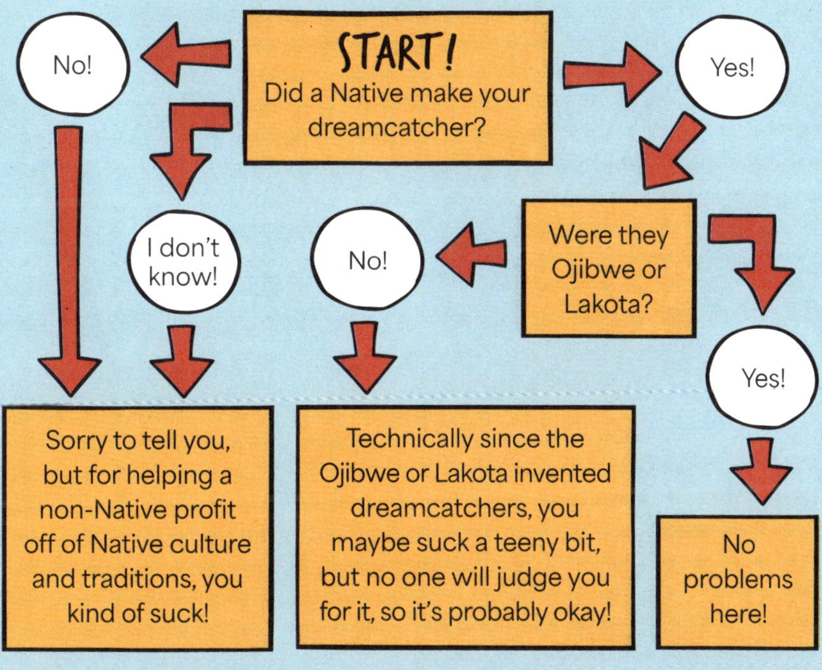

INDIGENOUS EXCELLENCE #2

Joe Medicine Crow

Joe Medicine Crow was a member of the Crow Tribe of Montana. He was the last War Chief of any of the more than thirty Great Plains tribes that make up a good chunk of the American Midwest. Based on that, you might think his prime was sometime in the Cowboys and Indians days of the 1800s. Nope! Joe lived until 2016, and his story is nuts!

Born in 1913, Joe Medicine Crow grew up on the Crow Indian Reservation. His step-grandfather was at the Battle of the Little Bighorn in 1876. Fun fact, this is the same battle where Indian killer General George Armstrong Custer was unalived by a bunch of Native folks from tribes including the Lakota, Cheyenne, and Arapaho. Custer was so despised that when the US Army recovered his body, the dead general reportedly had an arrow shoved up his penis. This is how much Natives hated that guy!

Artist's rendition

Joe Medicine Crow came from a long line of Crow War Chiefs and was taught that history and the importance of continuing the War Chief tradition. Being named War Chief isn't a job you send in a résumé for; it's something you earn. Here are the four specific steps you must complete in combat to become a War Chief of the Crow people:

1. Touch or strike the first enemy fallen, whether alive or dead
2. Wrestle a weapon away from an enemy warrior
3. Enter an enemy camp at night and steal a horse
4. Command a war party successfully

(National Park Service)

There wasn't a lot of combat happening on the Crow rez in the 1920s, so Joe took on a side quest. He was the first member of his tribe to receive a master's degree and became a schoolteacher for his people. That's already a career that most people would brag about for their whole lives, but Joe didn't stop there.

In 1941, Joe's main quest began. He enlisted in the army and traveled to Europe, where he spent much of World War II fighting Nazis and knocking out the four War Chief requirements.

While scouting in France, Joe ran into a lone German soldier. Instead of backing down, Joe put the boots to the soldier (#1), disarming him (#2) and taking him prisoner. He achieved the first two War Chief requirements in like ten minutes. Talk about a flex!

With the determination of a man trying to speedrun a game of *Super Mario 64*, Joe knocked out his third requirement when he led his fellow soldiers to blow up a German artillery nest, unlocking the "command a War Party" achievement (#4) with literal dynamite.

Now all Joe needed to do was sneak into an enemy camp and steal a horse. And this isn't rhetorical; it had to be a real *Mister Ed*-ass horse. Near the end of the war, Joe chased members of the SS into a farmhouse. Seeing horses penned up near the home, Joe snuck over the fence, climbed on a horse's back, and as his men opened fire on the SS, he rode that pony to safety. Here's how he described it:

. . . I looked at the horses. I had about forty or fifty head. I was riding a sorrel with a blaze, a real nice horse. So, I did something spontaneously. I sang a Crow praise song.

–Joe Medicine Crow
A Song for the Horse Nation: Horses in Native American Cultures

He didn't just steal one horse from the enemy, he stole FIFTY horses and he was so pumped about it he rocked out to a traditional Crow song as he did it (#3). When Joe returned to his reservation, he was officially named a War Chief by his people, and he spent the rest of his life giving lectures and helping found several organizations centered around remembering history and preserving the culture of his people.

He was so respected that there are several schools named after him. For his actions in World War II as well as his efforts to preserve his culture, he was awarded a Presidential Medal of Freedom by President Obama in 2009.

He also claims he was the first American soldier to set foot on German soil during the Second World War. Though this is hard to prove, it was later corroborated by his commanding officer, General Omar Bradley.

With all of the other cool stuff Joe did during the war, if you would have told me that he personally went back in time and shoved that arrow up Custer's urethra, I would have believed it.

WHAT SKIN TONE IS NATIVE?

We don't all look the same!

Western society has a tiny imagination for what Native people can look like, and much like John Wayne's hairline, it's all made up. A lot of that was caused by old cowboy movies featuring Native characters played largely by Italian actors. Their skin was literally painted to give them a red sheen.

Thanks to decades of straight up inaccurate Native representation, there's a little confusion about what skin color Native people actually are. I created this easy-to-follow skin tone chart to finally answer that age-old question!

From "white passing" to Afro-Indigenous and everything in between, Natives come in all colors, and we're all equally Native, bay-bee!

YOU'RE WELCOME #2

New York City

New York City, the Big Apple, the birthplace of Pizza Rat. It's one of the most influential cities in the world, and if you're wondering if the city and its culture wouldn't exist without Indigenous peoples, you're as right as the angles on the Brooklyn Bridge.

The island of Manhattan was originally the home of the Lenape people. The word "Manhattan" is even derived from the Lenape word "manahatta," meaning "island of many hills." If you've ever gotten sore calves hoofing it past 59th Street after gawking at lemurs at the Central Park Zoo, that translation makes way too much sense.

As the OGs of Manhattan, the Lenape helped the Dutch survive on the island in the early 1600s. The Dutch eventually realized, "Hey, we're colonizers," and decided to use their colonizer magic to force the Lenape off the land in a poorly explained real estate transaction. It's often reported that the Lenape traded the land for around twenty dollars' worth of beads, which isn't totally true. The gist is, the Lenape, not having the same concept of land ownership as the Dutch, thought they were making a deal for the "use" of the land, meaning they would all share it. The Dutch didn't bother to clarify the deal until they started building a wall around the southern tip of the island to keep the Dutch clogs in and the local Natives out. This was a total jerk move. It's kind of like if you signed a lease to live with a roommate and then the second you moved into your new apartment, you started building a wall around the kitchen and bathroom to keep your roommate from using it. The Lenape are still here, but due to forced relocation they've scattered into several different bands around the United States and Canada.

Yes, the entire United States is built on stolen land, but the land isn't the only contribution Native folks have to New York. They literally built the city too! It's almost like Native people doing a lot of the work and receiving none of the credit is kind of a pattern at this point. ANYWAY . . .

The Mohawk people, with aboriginal territory in upstate New York and parts of Ontario and Quebec, have a hardcore rite of passage where acts of courage and bravery are valued and an important part of entering into manhood. That used to involve traditional warrior stuff like fighting in war parties where collections of the toughest Mohawks teamed up to beat the asses of colonizers, opposing tribes, and that kind of thing. In the 1800s, that switched to building bridges and skyscrapers, because what's braver than standing hundreds of feet above a city on a girder and holding a rivet so hot it'd boil water in a second? (Literally nothing.)

By incorporating huge building construction into their core beliefs, the Mohawk people became respected steelworkers around the continent. They played a massive hand in building monumental structures like the Empire State Building, the Chrysler Building, the George Washington Bridge, and the Twin Towers. On September 11, 2001, Mohawk ironworkers were some of the first people to show up at Ground Zero to perform search and rescue duties, hours after the towers fell. There were so many Mohawk ironworkers in New York that they had their own neighborhood, called "Little Caughnawaga," which was around until the 1970s. I wish I had a time machine so I could travel there and buy a kana'tarokhón:we—cornbread so nutty it'd bring a tear to Mr. Peanut's eye.

In the local neighborhood bar, called "The Wigwam," there was even a sign that hung above the door that said, "The greatest ironworkers in the world pass through these doors."

In a balls-out awesome aside, the Mohawk people started referring to their ironworker tribal members as "Skywalkers." This was adopted from an Ottawa Tribe story published in the 1800s called *Ottawa the Sky Walker* about a young kid who walked into the sky. I don't have any concrete evidence that George Lucas lifted that term to name his *Star Wars* hero Luke Skywalker, but I mean, come on. Darth Vader means "Dark Father" in Dutch. George Lucas isn't exactly slick about hiding his real-world inspirations.

Okay, so New York was built by Indigenous peoples on land stolen by the Dutch from other Indigenous peoples. I could stop there and I would still have a compelling case for this "You're Welcome," but Natives are also responsible for the quintessential New York experience. No, I'm not talking about screaming "I'm walkin' here" at a taxi driven by the cast of *SNL*. Natives are responsible for greasy slices of New York pizza!

You're probably saying to yourself, "There's no way Natives invented pizza, that's clearly from Italy." To that I say, the best part of pizza is the marinara sauce, made of tomatoes, which were originally cultivated by Indigenous peoples of the Americas before being brought back to Italy in the 1600s. I rest my Indigenous case. Next time you're taking the D-train to 30 Rock, looking at a picture of the Statue of Liberty while thinking about what it'd be like if the Beastie Boys ever did improv at the Upright Citizens Brigade Theatre and washing those blessed Manhattan thoughts down with a New York slice and some extra-thick New York City hot chocolate, I have two words for you:

AN OPEN LETTER TO STEPHEN KING

Dear legendary horror author Stephen King,

Instead of using Indian burial grounds in your books, have you thought about using European burial grounds? Europe is terrifying! They spend all of their time inventing things to kill and torture people! I mean, look at the guillotine, a machine invented just to cut people's heads off; or "quartering," an execution technique where horses are used to rip someone apart; or the "pear of anguish," a metal, expandable torture device used to rip people's mouths and butts open. The European continent is way freakier than anything Natives ever did!

Take your book *Pet Sematary*. It's set on a spooky Indian burial ground that can bring dead things to life. That's nowhere near as scary as the Black Plague, which killed so many Europeans! You know what caused the Black Plague? Bad hygiene. The Medieval era alone was nasty. Instead of washing their hands, European folk did disgusting stuff to try to treat those plagues. One example was the "Vicary method," where they rubbed a plucked chicken's butt on the patient's plague wounds. That happened, and the "zombified Indian burial ground" thing for sure didn't.

Instead of leaning on mystical savage tropes and making up fake Native magic to up the scares in *It*, why don't you set it in Europe? The Paris catacombs are made of actual human bones. That's way creepier than anything Native people do. Plus, Belgian waffles are SCARY delicious.

The Shining is one of the scariest books of all time, and it takes place on tribal lands in Colorado. But you know what's scarier than tribal lands? Italy! So many people die in Italy that one town, Falciano del Massico, passed a decree in 2012 that made dying a crime because their cemetery was too full. Who do they plan on arresting? Ghosts?

What if instead of being in a house on an Indian burial ground, *The Amityville Horror* was in the Vatican? The Vatican is stuffed with the skeletons of former Catholic leaders and stolen Egyptian mummies. That alone is creepy, but it gets creepier when you realize that the Pope drinks blood and eats human flesh twice a day! He's basically real-life Nosferatu!

That's not the only spooky stuff the Catholic Church is up to. For years, they've collected the body parts of saints and showed them off as relics. There's also the decades of covering up child molestation by thousands of priests, but go off on Native ghosts being creepy, *I guess.*

Stephen King, I know *The Amityville Horror* wasn't written by you, but with its usage of Indian burial grounds as a trope to set up the story, it feels like something you wished you wrote.

Why do you hate us? Native cultures aren't scary. We're nice people! Plus, Indian burial grounds aren't real. Each tribe has their own burial practices, for sure, but they don't call them Indian burial grounds. Why would they? That's like if all of the cemeteries in Scotland

and Ireland were called "ginger burial grounds." That would be super weird!

And I get it. By including Indian burial grounds in your stories, you're actually saying that "settler guilt" is what's scary. A lot of people feel bad about the government's attempted genocide of Indigenous peoples. These tropes painting us as ghosts from the past are a coping mechanism for several centuries of Native blood on the hands of modern American society. Instead of using *us* to process that stuff, could you maybe try going to therapy? Or at the very least, make it a "Pilgrim burial ground" instead. Pilgrims' hats had buckles on them, which we can all agree that as a fashion choice is terrifying.

SECTION THREE

HONORS INDIAN TACOS

Now that you know the basics, you're ready to level up your NDN degree with rez-ucational topics like Pretendians, tribal casinos, boarding schools, and if Natives get free money from the government. (I wish!)

A LIST OF THINGS YOU CAN CALL A WORK MEETING THAT AREN'T A POWWOW!

Work meeting ≠ powwow

Most people who have to work Monday through Friday have heard the phrase "let's powwow about it," but have you ever considered how saying that actually sucks?

Though a ton of people think a powwow is a gathering of coworkers to talk about spreadsheets, quarterly profits, and if your company's upcoming merger is a good thing (it's not), a powwow isn't that at all. Powwows are an event for tribal communities to dance, eat a canoeload of frybread, and celebrate cultures that were almost taken from us. It would be kind of like if you said "let's Catholic Mass about it" to describe an HR meeting, which would be weirder than the Pope's big dumb hat!

Instead of calling your one-on-one with HR about how you used the puke emoji in the company Discord "a powwow," here are a list of terms you should use instead:

1. A work meeting
2. A job jamboree
3. A productivity party
4. A gathering of fellow employees
5. The Gathering of the Juggalos, but instead of Juggalos, it's coworkers
6. Burning Man, but the only thing burning is our passion for our jobs!
7. A huddle
8. A work-assigned task council
9. An employee convention

10. A "this could have been an email, but sorry it's in person" session
11. An office snack taste-testing challenge
12. A job-a-palooza
13. A work bris
14. An idea orgy
15. A congress of the collared shirts
16. Water Cooler Chitchat Part 2: This Time with No Water Cooler
17. A powwow. This one only works if your job has a powwow emcee, a host drum, people in regalia, and a sweaty uncle selling the best Indian tacos you've ever had in your life! Otherwise, don't use it!
18. A murder of crows, but instead of crows it's people and instead of murder it's a meeting
19. An "everyone in this room has a job" celebration
20. A money rally

Now, the next time you're at work and your boss tells you to powwow about it, please ask them to call it an "idea orgy" instead. You'd be helping all of us! Thank youuuuuu!

PICTURE QUIZ

Which living creatures does the United States government measure by blood quantum?

The answer won't shock you!

1. **Dogs?**

This three-legged rez dog is 50% pupper!

2. **Horses?**

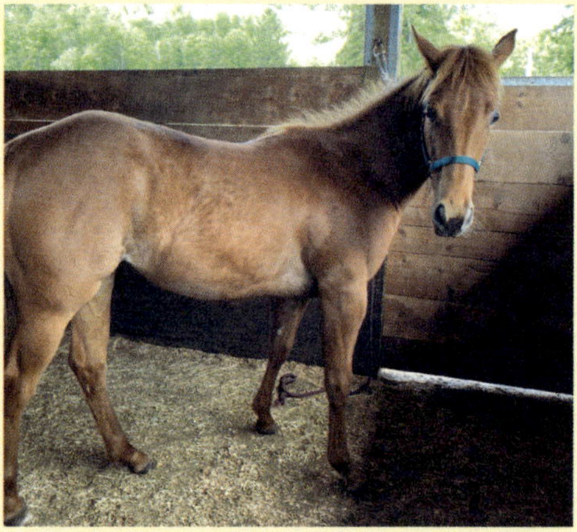

This adorable horse is 25% Secretariat!

3. Indians?

Look everyone! It's noted Sicangu Lakota tribal member Benny Wayne Sully!

TURN THE PAGE TO FIND OUT!

It's all three!

Weird, right? Native people are the only human race that the government measures by "blood percentages." It's the same way they evaluate purebred dogs and horses, and it's been that way since the early 1700s' "Indian Blood Law." Why would they rate Indians the same way they rate a Thoroughbred stallion? It's not because we're good runners!

It boils down to optics. If the government can convince people we're less than human, they can justify stealing our lands, killing us, and in general treating us like we don't matter. Remember when I mentioned that we're called "merciless Indian Savages" in the Declaration of Independence? That's not how you'd describe someone you respect or think you should treat as an equal. It's a cog in a larger machine that ends with Indigenous folks getting screwed, and not in that good way.

Blood quantum, as it's called, is a big part of that system. It's what people are referring to when they say they're "one-sixteenth Cherokee." Back in the buckled shoe days, Natives could not legally be United States citizens. The Indian Blood Law was to decide who was Native and who was white! If you had a certain percentage of Native blood, you didn't have rights. Native people couldn't obtain United States citizenship until 1924 with the signing of the Indian Citizenship Act, so this went on for a LONG time!

With 1934's Indian Reorganization Act, things flipped like a vinyl record, and instead of Native blood percentages dictating your United States citizenship, it dictated your tribal citizenship. The US government told tribal governments that their members had to have a certain percentage—for example, one fourth "Indian blood" (one Native grandparent)—to be an enrolled member of the tribe. It's all part of a system designed to deny Native people our treaty rights.

That, to me, is one of the sadder things about this stuff. When our tribes signed these treaties, it was presumably in good faith and with the expectation that the government would keep its promises. Like a construction worker building an NFL stadium, the government kept moving the goal posts, sometimes for over a hundred years, to avoid giving tribes what the government is obligated to give. It's like if you borrow twenty dollars from a friend, but instead of giving them the money you owe them, you tell them to meet you fifty miles out of town, and then when they show up, you text them and say, "Oh, sorry, I meant a million miles out of town." Your friend would be right to be mad at you!

When the Indian Reorganization Act passed, there was a push for the government to actually start giving tribes what they promised in their treaty agreements. So it became pricier to have more federally recognized Native people entitled to those benefits. The plan was that if you set a blood percentage requirement for someone to be an enrolled member of a tribe—one-eighth, for example—eventually when enough Native folks have kids with people who aren't tribal members, there won't be anyone with enough Indian blood left to claim benefits.

This is what's often referred to as a "paper genocide," where instead of killing us off literally, they're killing us off statistically. But the end goal is the same: to get rid of us like a week-old, overripe avocado.

A way for us to fight that stuff is through tracking our enrollment to show the federal government that our tribes are still around and flourishing. This is done partly because tribes are their own governmental bodies and it's good to know who your citizens are, and partly because, by proving that we are still a flourishing people, we have legal grounds to force the government to give us what it owes us. Like an easily distracted four-year-old, the government is awful at keeping its promises, so we've got to remind them all the time, which isn't exhausting at all. (Wait, yes it is.)

HOW TO DRESS "LIKE AN INDIAN" FOR HALLOWEEN

Non-Natives love dressing like "Indians" for Halloween, and the costumes are always racist and bad! If you want to dress like an Indian without getting beat up, here's an easy guide. And if you're wondering if this is the exact outfit I'm wearing right now, it is!

ENROLLED, UNENROLLED, AND ENROLLMENT-CURIOUS!

How tribes get to choose who their members are

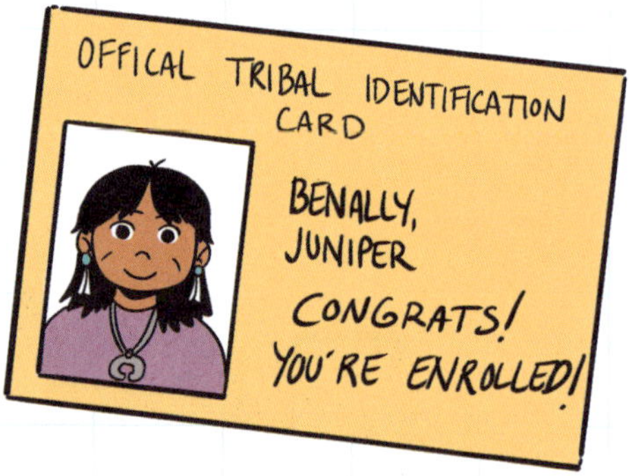

Earlier, I explained that tribes are their own sovereign nations within the United States. The technical term is "domestic dependent nations" who have the right to self-govern. What that means is, tribes get to decide who is or isn't a member.

If you're "enrolled" it means you're legally a member of a tribal nation in the same way that you might be a citizen of a country. When I say I'm "enrolled Cowlitz," I mean I'm a citizen of my tribe. I have a tribal ID card and everything. It's like a driver's license, but instead of giving me permission to drive, it gives me a 15% discount at the Starbucks in my tribe's casino. It rocks. Since tribes are their own sovereign nations, all the five-hundred-plus federally recognized and hundreds of state-recognized tribes handle the enrollment process differently, but most tribes use one of two methods.

Blood Quantum: I covered this a little bit in a previous chapter, but that was just a scratch. Now, we're diving all the way into the deep cuts of the blood quantum discourse. Also, I'm aware that "blood quantum" sounds like a bad James Bond movie sequel, but that's not all that it is. It's a specific metric that's been lorded over Natives for over a hundred years. In the early 1900s, the government was doing everything they could to assimilate Indigenous folks into their colonial view of society. One way they did this is they promised every Native head of household a plot of land. Native societies tend to be more communal, so they thought that by giving each Native person their own land to cultivate, it'd make them more individualistic and less focused on community. (Basically, they tried to make us super greedy.)

The problem was, a lot of non-Natives came out of the woodwork, claiming Native identity to get what they thought was free land. The United States Government decided to create "rolls," like the Dawes Roll, to make a list of all Native people of any given tribe. This established the baseline of who is considered to be a full-blooded tribal member. When someone says they're one-eighth Cherokee, it means their great-grandparent was on one of these rolls. If both of your parents are on these rolls, congrats. You're a full-blooded member of your tribe. If three of your grandparents are "full-blooded" but one isn't, your blood quantum is three-fourths. Different tribes have different BQ requirements, with some requiring as much as five-eighths BQ (five full-blooded great-grandparents) and some requiring as little as one thirty-second BQ (one full-blooded great-great-great-grandparent). And despite how many times I used "great" in the last sentence, this whole thing is anything but!

If you're looking for anyone to blame for this mess, I recommend United States senator from Massachusetts Henry L. Dawes. He introduced the Dawes Act in 1887 in an attempt to assimilate Native people into Western society. (Side note: President Coolidge's administration researched the effects of the Dawes Act in the 1920s, and they found that it was mainly used to do the one thing Americans love doing more than freebasing hot dogs—that's right, screwing Native peoples out of our lands.)

Dawes died over a hundred years ago, so it's impossible to beat him up over this. Instead, I'll beat him up comedically with this picture of him wearing a dunce cap.

If Dawes was alive, he'd be so humiliated right now!

Lineal Descent: Tribes that don't use blood quantum often use what's called "lineal descent" or "lineage" to decide who can or can't be enrolled in their tribe. Lineal descent basically means that if one of your parents is an enrolled member of your tribe, you can be enrolled too.

This creates an unbroken lineage of tribal citizens, traced all the way back to the original members of the tribe on whatever documents were originally used when the tribe received recognition. Some tribes that use lineal descent have specific requirements, like for example, matriarchal descent, meaning that you can only be enrolled in your tribe if your mother is an enrolled member. Lineal descent is all pretty simple, and I didn't even have to use a picture of Henry L. Dawes covered in stink lines to prove my point.

Tribal citizenship is only partially biological. It's not something simple like a birth certificate; it's written proof that you are part of your community. Anyone who tries to boil Native identity down to just blood is actively eroding our sovereignty as self-governing nations and is not someone you should listen to.

It's why, when Senator Elizabeth Warren used a DNA test to try to "prove tribal citizenship" a few years ago, it was clowned on by Native folks so hard. As far as I can tell, 23andMe isn't a tribe. And if it were, their frybread would be bland as hell.

My tribe uses lineal descent to determine enrollment eligibility. I'm Native because I am Cowlitz. I'm Cowlitz because my mother is Cowlitz and had me enrolled in our tribe. I can track my tribal lineage back to a specific Cowlitz ancestor who is shared by many other members of my tribe. My community claims me on our enrollment records, and I am, in an official and documented way, a citizen of my tribal nation, but also, every time I go to my tribe's casino, someone I don't know tells me they're my cousin and tries to bum twenty dollars off of me. If there's a more earnest way to be claimed by a community, I don't want to hear it.

One caveat to all of this is that being an enrolled member isn't the be-all end-all answer to if someone is Native or not. There are people who are part of a tribe biologically and deeply involved in their communities who fall through the cracks of enrollment. Those reasons range from "their ancestor made a typo on their enrollment paperwork" to "when many of these rolls were made, it was legal to murder Natives, so some Natives recorded a different race on the census so as not to get killed by the United States government." Multi-tribal citizens (people in more than one tribe), freedmen, and adopted tribal members further complicate things.

All of that's to say, like any government, a tribe dictates who its citizens are, but when you try to cram an Indigenous system of community over colonial ideas of citizenship, it's not going to be a perfect solution.

It's nuanced for sure, but personally, I'd rather that tribes be in charge of defining their membership. That system has its share of problems too, like disenrollment and preferred treatment of some members over others. Because tribes are ultimately collections of fallible people, things like colorism, racism, and anti-Blackness can also play a role in some (but not all) tribes' enrollment decisions. It's an uncomfortable subject, and it sucks that it's a thing because Natives come in all colors.

That said, if I had a choice between having my cousin control my citizenship or a separate government that spent several hundred years trying to kill me, I'd choose my cousin every time. The only thing he's ever tried to kill me at is *Super Mario Kart,* and baby, I'm still standing.

SO, YOU'RE DISTANTLY RELATED TO A CHEROKEE PRINCESS

A haiku

Oftentimes people will claim Native identity by saying that one of their great-great-great-grandparents was a Cherokee princess. This easy-to-read haiku is for them.

So, the Cherokee

Don't have princesses. Sorry!

You're not Cherokee.

This is a Cherokee princess riding a unicorn to show that neither of those things are real, nor is your Cherokee princess relative.

FLOWCHART: ARE YOU A PRETENDIAN?

If an Indian is someone who is Indigenous to North America, a "Pretendian" is that, but the liar version. Pretendians are folks who use a made-up Native identity to take jobs and opportunities meant for actual Native folks. They are all too common in the United States and Canada, with everyone from college professors to actors to famous musicians being outed for claiming fake Native identities. It's always embarrassing and causes a lot of damage and mistrust in tribal communities. Every time a Pretendian is outed (which happens often!), I throw up in my mouth a little bit.

If you think you or one of your friends might be faking being Native for their own personal gain, here's a flowchart to help you get to the bottom of it like a Pretendian trying to get to the bottom of a college scholarship application meant for actual Natives.

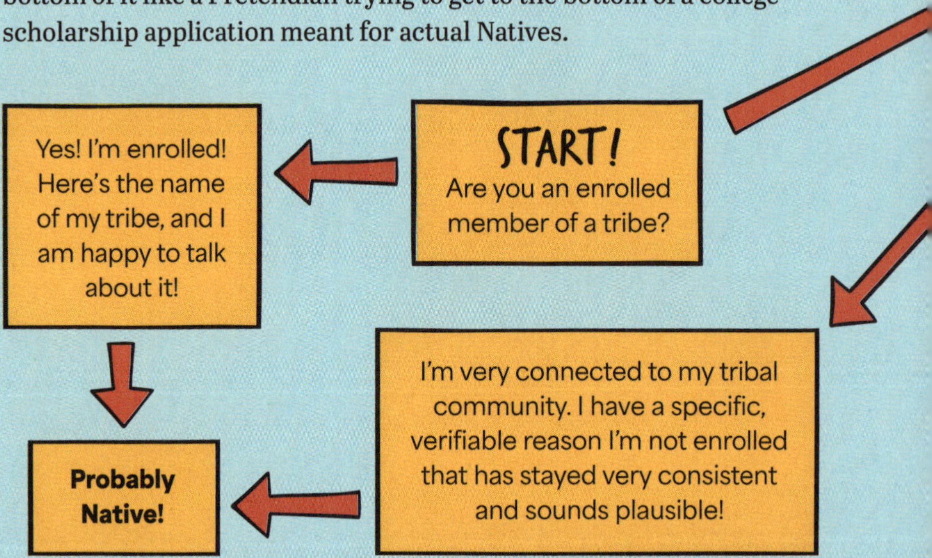

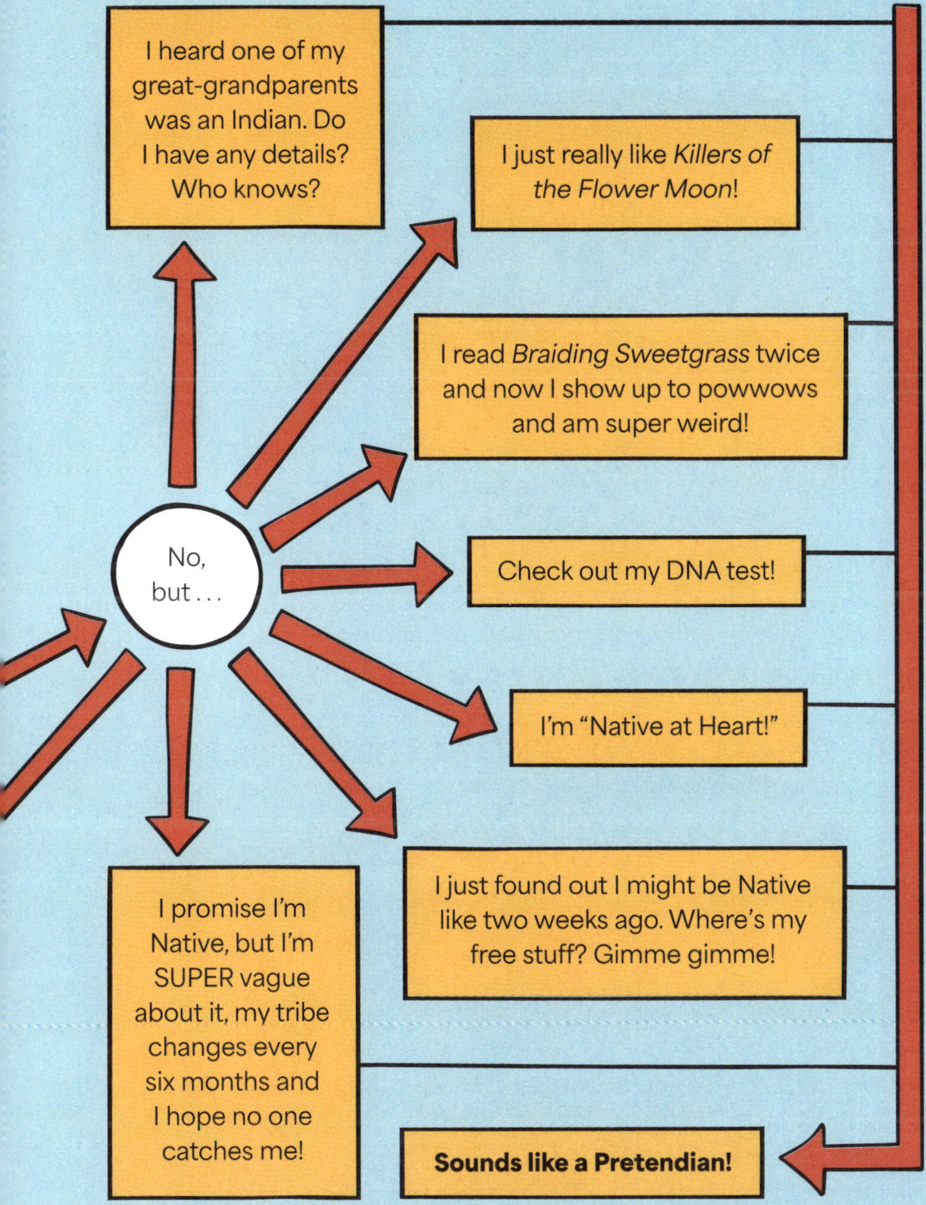

Author Note: "Pretendian" is an in-group term that can be a little uncomfortable when non-Natives throw it around. Please don't go Pretendian-hunting on our behalf. That would be unhelpful and weird!

SACRED FAILS #1

Stop burning all of our sage!

I get it. Native people are full of sage wisdom and more sacred than an eagle riding a jet ski while playing a flute. It's no surprise that non-Natives love to copy our mystical ways, but would you believe that when they copy us, they always do it wrong and mess it up? I can, and when it happens it's not a regular failure, it's a Sacred Fail.

Burning white sage, or "smudging," has become a popular practice for woo-woo spiritual New Ager types. It's so popular that you can buy bundles of sage easily at the most sacred store of all, Urban Outfitters. Despite what you've heard, burning sage to clear out bad energy wasn't invented by wine moms in Iowa. It was originated by Indigenous peoples across the Americas, who burn sage as part of our spiritual practices, and a lot of Native folks still participate in this practice. Or at least we did, until all the non-Natives started copying us and burning it so they could feel "closer to the Earth" or whatever.

Like a Labubu that is currently on fire, burning white sage has become such a fad for non-Natives that the plant is now endangered in some states. Many of these sage-selling big-box stores, who say they harvest their "ethnically sourced" sage "naturally," often purchase it from non-Native sellers. In some cases, these sellers literally break into tribal lands and illegally rip the sage out of tribal gardens, stealing a plant that many Native people depend on for our spirituality. It's like if, all of a sudden, drinking sacramental wine got so popular that there wasn't enough left over for Catholics to use for their Sunday Mass. It sucks, and the Rancho Cucamonga Police Department alone reportedly busts dozens of white sage poachers per year. These poachers steal a combined hundreds of pounds of sage from tribal lands to sell to "spiritual" shops.

Even if you take the cultural appropriation out of it, it was illegal for years for Native people to participate in our spiritual practices. That includes things like sage burning, accessing our sacred sites on federal land, and owning sacred objects like eagle feathers. All of that changed when the American Indian Religious Freedom Act passed in 1978. It's nuts that in 1977 it was legal to have a "Jedi-themed wedding" at your local church, but burning sage would have gotten you in trouble with the law. Many Native elders were sent to jail and died practicing this kind of thing. Now, only a couple decades later, burning white sage is such a fad that Native people can't practice it because there's hardly any left.

Now that sage is harder to come by, Native people have to fight with someone who heard about smudging on TikTok over the last three bundles left over at your local crystal shop that doubles as a Coffee Bean. Sage crops have been over-harvested by non-Natives, driving up prices, and now Native people effectively pay a double tax to follow our own spiritual practices. It sure ain't Native people's fault that it's gotten this messy.

And for clarity, when I say "messy," I'm not talking about the fact that post-smudging, there's sage residue everywhere. That kind of messy I don't mind.

If burning sage makes you feel better about yourself, I get it. It's powerful medicine. But could you maybe replace burning sage with burning a pair of Lululemon yoga pants? It's not like basic Midwest suburban moms are going to run out of yoga pants. Plus, those are mostly made of plastic and petroleum, and Americans love burning that stuff! Since they've burned so much of our sage, it would be a great way to turn this Sacred Fail into a sacred win!

Smells like a sacred win to me!!

TREATIES AND YOU!

Or, why you should stop complaining about Natives getting benefits from the government!

Indians get free stuff from the government.

–Some dork

One of the most common stereotypes heaped upon Native folks, aside from our dashing good looks (true!), is the claim that we're always getting government handouts (not true!). I can assure you that the government isn't sending bags of free Indian money to my house, but if they were, that money wouldn't be free. Also, if the government was giving free money to Natives, who would they even give it to? Do people with one-half blood quantum get half as much, or do they drive a truck full of cash to Wes Studi's house and tell him to figure it out? He is trustworthy in a fatherly sort of way, but that's too much work for even him.

The reason some believe that we get free money is a word that a lot of Native folks are familiar with: "treaties." As I've mentioned in previous chapters, tribes are their own federally or state-recognized sovereign nations within the United States. We have our own constitutions, political figures, languages, and systems of governance. A "treaty" is a formal agreement between two or more governments—for example, the United States and the Navajo Nation.

Treaties between the federal government and tribal nations aren't new. One of the first of these treaties is the Jay Treaty of 1794, which allows Indigenous people born in Canada to cross the border and live and work in the United States without needing a visa. There are still a ton of Canadian First Nations folks who benefit from this treaty, and they deserve it! For many tribes, the Canada-US border split their tribal lands in half. This treaty is a VERY rare case of colonial governments understanding that the border crossed us and they should give Indigenous folks this tiny exception.

In total, the United States government made around four hundred treaties with different tribes between 1778 and 1871. Though some of those treaties, like the Treaty of Fort Pitt in 1778, were logistical agreements allowing the United States Army to travel through tribal lands, once the United States started spilling Manifest Destiny juice all over the continent, things got rougher around the edges. With the government forcing Native folks off of their traditional homelands, these treaties became something a little closer to land deals. Now, oftentimes these treaties were made at gunpoint, so to say that tribal leaders were coerced "under duress" would be a severe understatement. But they were still legally binding contracts—"if you give us your land, we'll give you something in return"—which is such a basic concept that even a literal toddler should be able to understand it.

In the same way that every legally binding contract is unique, every treaty is different, but I like to think of them as being like an apartment lease. In this case, the tenant is the United States. Usually, what the United States offered as "rent" in these treaties to different tribal nations was reservation land, protection, healthcare, education, goods, additional fishing and hunting rights, and the "right to self-governance," meaning that tribes generally don't have to abide by state laws.

That doesn't mean reservations are lawless places where anything goes (because tribal police do exist; there's a whole show about it called *Dark Winds,* and it rocks), but we do get some extra benefits here and there. Tribal members often receive free admittance to state parks, as well as free or discounted hunting licenses on our aboriginal territories. In many states, it's illegal to possess things like eagle feathers and bear claws, but enrolled Native folks can own them without issue. Because they don't have to abide by state laws, reservations are also great places to buy fireworks of questionable legality. That's not a cultural thing; it's just a fun loophole that I hope never closes.

These are all concessions that the government has given to us. If we're our own sovereign nations within the United States, we should be allowed to participate in our cultures without fear of being arrested and also blow up a small part of our reservation whenever we want.

Additionally, the government is "morally and legally obligated" to fund things like Indian Health Services, which helps run tribal clinics for Native folks across the country, and the Bureau of Indian Education, which is meant to help fund schools on reservations.

These clinics probably aren't going to suck out your buccal fat, but they provide free or reduced-cost basic health care for Native folks. I received most of my K-12 education at tribally run schools on the Tulalip rez. I even had my wisdom teeth yanked out at a tribal clinic, so I can vouch for how vital these services are for tribal communities.

Before you applaud the government for being nice to us Indians, you should know that these services are often underfunded, understaffed, and are usually one of the first things on the chopping block for politicians looking to balance the budget. When it comes to treaty obligations, the government tries to weasel out of them ALL. THE. TIME.

Only a few decades after signing the Treaty of Fort Pitt with the Lenape people, the United States government had already broken their treaty, forcing the Lenape off of their traditional lands.

The Fort Laramie Treaty of 1868 promised the Black Hills of South Dakota to the Sioux people as part of the Great Sioux Reservation. It took the United States government six years before they broke that treaty, sending the Army into the Black Hills to kick the Sioux out because General Custer discovered gold in the area. If there's one thing that makes colonizers get all genocidal, it's the gold in them thar hills.

The Black Hills are a sacred site to the Sioux people, and this led to several battles between the Sioux and the Army, including the Battle of the Little Bighorn, where Custer notably got an arrow jammed up his penis.

Okay, bringing that up again was a low blow, but much like the arrow in General Custer's penis, I had to jam that in there. Suck it, Custer!

Over a hundred years later, the Supreme Court ruled that the Black Hills had been illegally taken from the Sioux in the 1980 court case *United States v. Sioux Nation of Indians*. The US government was ordered to pay one hundred million dollars in compensation for the stolen land.

In a true "Indigenous real one" move, the Oglala Sioux rejected the money because the land was never for sale in the first place. The legal battle over the land continues to this day. To add insult to injury, the Black Hills also contains "Mount Rushmore," that famous monument featuring four presidents' faces blasted onto the side of a mountain (gross). It's like if someone stole your car and when they tried to return it years later, it had Jared Leto's Joker airbrushed on the side of it, which I think we can all agree would be the worst!

This is a few of many examples of the United States honoring treaties only until the second they discovered gold or decided they want to build an oil pipeline or railroad through tribal lands they no longer had legal title to. Funny how that works, huh?

Earlier in this chapter, I mentioned that around four hundred treaties between the government and tribes were written, but that doesn't mean that there are around four hundred active treaties. Around 350 of those treaties were actually ratified. If you think that smells like some grade A bullshit, take a whiff and gag, because it for sure ain't roses.

In many cases, the person sent to negotiate these treaties tore up the treaty after negotiations finished. When this happened, the tribes were rarely informed that their deal wasn't being honored, and they'd operate assuming they had a legal treaty until the Army showed up. Wonder why some Natives have trust issues with the government? It's stuff like this!

Though these treaties are, in some cases, hundreds of years old, none of them have an expiration date. They're still active and upholding them is a constant legal fight. It's all so complicated that some lawyers specialize in Indian law, battling the government on behalf of tribes to make sure their treaty obligations, which they are still VERY much entitled to, are met. And these cases aren't rare. There have been dozens of lawsuits over even the past few years where tribes sued state and federal governments over unmet treaty obligations, and every year a handful of these cases even make it to the Supreme Court.

People who are opposed to treaties often use the defense that Native folks should "get over it" and "these treaties are so old that we shouldn't have to honor them anymore," but that's the dumbest take. The United States Constitution was signed in the 1700s and is still used as the basis for the USA's legal system. The Doctrine of Discovery, written in the 1400s, is still used as legal precedent in several countries, including the United States. Many parts of the Magna Carta, written around eight hundred years ago, are still part of English law.

If you've lived in the same apartment for a few years, you don't get to stop paying your rent because your lease is old. To think that the United States doesn't have to pay for their treaty obligations because "they've paid enough already" is an argument by people who don't know what they're talking about, and that's not just me talking. The Supreme Court said basically the same thing when they sided with the Muscogee Nation in the 2020 case *McGirt v. Oklahoma*. Justice Gorsuch wrote this fire opening line in his majority opinion in that case:

> On the far end of the Trail of Tears was a promise. Forced to leave their ancestral lands in Georgia and Alabama, the Creek Nation received assurances that their new lands in the West would be secure forever. . . . Today we are asked whether the land these treaties promised remains an Indian reservation for purposes of federal criminal law. Because Congress has not said otherwise, we hold the government to its word.
>
> –Justice Neil Gorsuch
> *McGirt v. Oklahoma*

Besides guaranteeing himself a front-row seat at any powwow he wants for life, Gorsuch also solidified some fantastic legal precedent, underlining that these treaties are forever obligations.

Side note: Gorsuch, a conservative Supreme Court Justice, isn't someone many people would suspect of being a champion of Native rights, but he truly is. Part of the reason is that before he served on the Supreme Court, he ruled over a ton of Indian law cases and became educated about our struggles. The justices who vote against us usually don't have any experience within Indian country. It turns out that regardless of political affiliation, when people learn about us, they tend to treat us like we're human beings. Who woulda thought?

So, TL;DR: Yes, some tribes do get benefits from the government. No, this money is not "free." In fact, these small entitlements are only signifying the US paying their end of the lease. A tiny number of Natives receive "per capita" payments as a share of revenue from their tribal businesses, but that's not from the government. It's from their tribes, and those payments are often subject to federal income tax (you're welcome).

It's not like the government's sending no-strings-attached checks to all Native people, but if they were, mind your own business. If you have a problem with any of this, you could always give us all our land back.

TWENTY-SIX REASONS WHY MY TRIBE'S CASINO RULES!

A great thing about tribal sovereignty is, it lets us run businesses on our lands that otherwise may be restricted in a given state. For example, tribal casinos! The Oneida Tribe tested this out in the 1970s by operating bingo games on their lands in Wisconsin. Other tribes followed, and like sometimes-bad-but-in-this-case-good relatives, the Supreme Court affirmed tribal gaming rights in the 1987 case *California v. Cabazon Band of Mission Indians*.

All of this paved the way for my tribe to flex our sweet, sweet sovereignty and open our Ilani Casino Resort in 2017 just north of Portland, Oregon. Here are a bunch of reasons why Ilani is so awesome:

1. The bathrooms are sparkling clean!
2. Ilani has over a dozen restaurants and bars, including a burger place that has a wall decorated with four bedazzled cow skulls!

3. Our hotel is the tallest building in Clark County, Washington!
4. The hit 2000s band Hoobastank recently played a concert at one of our chain restaurants!
5. The casino is owned by my tribe and as a Cowlitz tribal member, I technically kind of own part of it!
6. If you're a Platinum Club member, you can get complimentary rooms in our Four Diamond hotel!
7. The lights outside our casino are so bright that it's occasionally a danger to local wildlife!
8. Many of the design elements of Ilani are inspired by Cowlitz culture and regalia, further establishing the beauty of my tribe's traditions and highlighting that we've been a part of the region since time immemorial and we will continue to be for millennia to come.
9. On one side of our hotel, the rooms overlook my tribe's aboriginal territory, including Mount St. Helens, which we call Lawetlat'la in Cowlitz!
10. On the other side of our hotel, the rooms overlook our Cowlitz-owned weed dispensary!
11. Profits from our Cowlitz businesses help give us resources to fund culture and language programs to preserve traditions that were in serious danger of disappearing due to years of colonization and attempted genocide, as well as scholarship and benefit programs meant to help tribal members flourish in our lives and careers.
12. We're like a twenty-minute drive from Portland, Oregon!
13. The road to our casino from I-5 features TWO roundabouts!
14. Starting in the mid-1800s, my tribe fought for generations to receive our federal recognition and finally earned it in 2000. I can still remember my mom telling me the news with tears in her eyes. To me, our casino and businesses are a testament to the enduring spirit of my people and the beautiful Indigenous mindset that you're not only working to make your life better, but also to make your great-great-great-grandkids' lives better.
15. The bread at our steakhouse is delicious!

16. The appetizers at our steakhouse are delicious!
17. The steaks at our steakhouse are delicious (obviously)!
18. The profits from Ilani don't only help tribal members! We also give to the local community in a real way, employing approximately one thousand local community members and donating resources and equipment to nearby towns! Our tribe often preaches the "potlatch spirit" of generosity. A potlatch is a Pacific Northwest tribal "giving ceremony" where the host tribe shares their wealth by bestowing gifts upon allies and friends. It's amazing to see our tribe able to continue that spirit in the modern day with the help of our business ventures. Plus, who doesn't love a party where you get a present for showing up!
19. Our hotel is filled with art purchased from Cowlitz artists!
20. Our "culture corridor" connecting our hotel and casino allows patrons to learn about our people, culture, and shared history!
21. We've won so many awards for being one of the best casinos in Washington that we'd need another casino to store them!
22. I often use Ilani as an example of tribal capitalism, proving that money in the right hands and distributed properly, instead of hoarded by a single person, can act like the best form of socialism. Every dollar spent at a tribe-owned business goes into the local community, tribal or otherwise.
23. We've had our casino for a short time, but it's illuminated for me all the good that happens when Native people and tribal communities are allowed to build our own economic engines. By having successful businesses of our own, we have a greater say in local politics and decisions that affect not just our tribe but the whole region. Seeing politicians from my tribe standing alongside the governor of our state and knowing that they see each other as equals fills me with pride because I know the struggles we faced to have a seat at that table.
24. It's made me happy for the success of other tribes too, because if their businesses are flourishing, I know firsthand the good it's doing for their peoples and preserving their cultures.

25. Also, I feel ridiculously fortunate. Less than half of the tribes in the United States have their own casinos. Part of it is due to location. Many reservations are in rural areas, far from population centers. Our reservation is next to a big city, a great location for a casino, and we had the right help and access to resources at the right time to build something like Ilani. All things considered, our tribe is doing great. Every tribe isn't so lucky, and I hope we casino tribes can all help tribes less fortunate than us in their financial journeys too, because our tribes are stronger together than apart.
26. If I show my tribal ID card at our in-casino video arcade, I get a 10% discount on credits. I try not to be too smug about it while playing *Dance Dance Revolution*, but I'm bad at hiding how I feel!

COOL MOMENTS IN INDIGENOUS HISTORY #3

Redbone getting banned from United States radio and still creating a number one hit song!

If you have functioning ears and have left your house in the past fifty years, chances are high you've listened to the band Redbone. One of the first all-Native rock bands, Redbone formed in the 1960s and spent the '70s Redboning powwow-influenced funk music all over the Billboard charts. Director James Gunn even used their biggest hit, "Come and Get Your Love," as the theme to the *Guardians of the Galaxy* trilogy, but their second-biggest hit was basically banned from US radio.

That song was called "We Were All Wounded at Wounded Knee," off of their 1973 album *Wovoka*. It was about the Wounded Knee Massacre of 1890, where the United States Army attacked a peaceful camp of Lakota people in Wounded Knee, South Dakota. Around three hundred Lakota, many of them defenseless women and children, were murdered by the Army in that massacre. It's occasionally referred to as the "Battle of Wounded Knee," but anyone trying to frame it as a "battle" is selling you a bill of goods (and those goods smell suspiciously like bullshit).

The Wounded Knee Massacre looms large for Indigenous folks as an example of the cruelty of the United States government, who attacked the camp to suppress the Lakota from simply practicing their culture. Over eighty years later, Redbone wrote a song about the massacre, including the rippling effects it had on them and the Native activists of the present day. "We were all wounded at Wounded Knee" is repeated as the song's chorus to remind us that the effects of that event still linger. They were trying to keep the memory of this tragedy alive, wrapped in a fantastic 1970s funk package.

Unfortunately, Redbone's record label, CBS, reacted to it like Dracula reacting to a smelly loaf of garlic bread. They were worried that by pointing out the United States' genocidal centuries-long treatment of Native people, the song was too "controversial," and refused to release it, which effectively banned it from United States radio.

Still believing in the song, Redbone bassist Pat Vegas allegedly snuck into the business CBS used to print records and had them make five hundred copies of the song. He smuggled those records to Europe, where it became a number one hit, and it's no surprise. The song is such a banger!

Now, decades later, fans around the world are campaigning for Redbone to be inducted into the Rock and Roll Hall of Fame, and that CBS record exec who refused to release the song is in the Pants-Peeing Coward Hall of Fame. The latter hall of fame used to have a physical location, but it floated away on account of all of the pee. Whoops!

A PROPOSAL FOR MUSEUMS AND UNIVERSITIES THAT HAVE LARGE COLLECTIONS OF NATIVE ARTIFACTS OR REMAINS

Hello,

If you're a museum or university curator with Indigenous artifacts or the literal bones of Indigenous people in your collections, I have a simple one-step proposal for you.

1. **Give it back.**

Thank you for reading!

YOU'RE WELCOME

NO ONE HATED ANYTHING MORE THAN GALVARINO HATED THE CONQUISTADORS

As you've probably guessed, Indigenous people aren't fans of colonization. Maybe it's all the cruelty, rape, murder, stealing of our lands, and taking away of our cultures? If you've ever wondered, "Which Indigenous person hates colonization the most?" I have an answer for you. His name was Galvarino, he was a chieftain of the Mapuche people in what is now called Chile in the 1500s, and he DESPISED the conquistadors.

After Columbus "discovered" the Americas, the Spanish monarchy got colonization fever and sent even more genocidal freaks across the Atlantic to the "New World." They were called the conquistadors, and they invaded parts of the Americas all throughout the sixteenth and seventeenth centuries.

One of the ways they'd intimidate local tribes is, after capturing a tribe's warriors, they'd cut the warriors' hands off before sending them back to their villages. The warriors' missing limbs were a constant reminder of the conquistadors' monstrously bad vibes.

After the 1557 Battle of Lagunillas between the conquistadors and the Mapuche, Galvarino was captured and one of his hands was sliced off. Instead of letting them intimidate him for even a second, he put his other hand on the chopping block, telling the conquistadors to cut that off too. The vast majority of in-person accounts of this say that when the conquistadors cut off both of Galvarino's hands, he didn't even flinch.

With the Mapuche hobbled, the conquistadors thought that when they came back a few weeks later the tribe would quickly surrender. What they didn't expect was an army of absolutely furious Mapuche, with Galvarino at the front of the line with freaking BLADES tied to his handless wrists.

This was the Battle of Millarapue, and though there were a couple of people there documenting the event (most notably Spanish poet Alonso de Ercilla and historian Jerónimo de Vivar), this happened over five hundred years ago, so it's tough to parse the legend from reality. Some historians say Galvarino tied "lances" to his stumps, others say it was swords or knives. One thing that's consistent is that he was the absolute front of the front lines, and he destroyed at least one conquistador officer with his wrist blades like he was Wolverine from the X-Men ripping apart a Sentinel.

The battle ended with Galvarino's capture, but he was such a fierce warrior that Alonso de Ercilla begged the Spanish to let Galvarino join the conquistadors. In response, Galvarino said he'd rather be executed, challenging the conquistadors to do it with this insane line:

> **If anyone is squeamish about taking this vital step, he has not taken on board the mutilation, with these teeth and lopped-off arms.**
>
> –Galvarino
> *The Araucana* (translated by David Russell)

Right?! He basically said, "If you don't execute me, I will murder you with my teeth." I cry like a baby when H Mart sells out of my favorite peach-flavored seltzer water. I can't imagine saying THAT right before being executed.

Though Galvarino didn't survive the battle, his hatred of Spanish colonization became a rallying cry for the Mapuche. The conquistadors spent over 180 years after that trying to enslave the Mapuche, but through grit and determination, the Mapuche held them off. They were one of the only tribes in South America that, over hundreds of years of colonization, were never conquered by the Spanish empire, which is so Indigenous AF that it makes me sweat thinking about it.

Galvarino was such a hero that three hundred years after his death, the people of Chile named a city after him that stands to this day.

Now, whenever anyone asks me how much Indigenous people hate colonization, I show them a picture of Galvarino, the dude who hated colonization so much he literally ran into battle with blades tied to his handless wrists. Then I cry a little bit because oh god that had to hurt.

THESE PEOPLE AREN'T INVITED TO THE POWWOW #3

The Pope

The history of European colonization across planet Earth has villains galore, but they don't get much bigger, badder, and pointy-hat-ier than the leader of the Catholic Church, the Pope! For creating a framework that gave legal permission for half a millennium of colonization and the murder of hundreds of millions of Indigenous people, the Pope isn't just not invited to the powwow, he's not allowed at Indian markets or any bison chili cookoffs either.

You're probably wondering why Indigenous people feel a certain way about an old man who rides around in a car called the "popemobile." For that, I point to the 1400s papal bull, or decree from the Pope, called "Inter Caetera." As the religious leader of the Catholic Church, the Pope was often brought in as a mediator when big-time European monarchs had disputes. When Europeans began exploring other continents, there were arguments among European nobility about who actually had colonizer dibs on the newly "discovered" lands.

To solve that problem and to keep the olde timey European monarchy group chat happy, Pope Nicholas V and Pope Alexander VI made a series of decrees, establishing that Spain had all rights to the "New World" (i.e., the Americas) and that any land that hadn't already been claimed by Christians was up for grabs for any Christian-led nations that wanted it. It also included this garbage line:

> *Among other works well pleasing to the Divine Majesty and cherished of our heart, this assuredly ranks highest, that in our times especially the Catholic faith and the Christian religion be exalted and be everywhere increased and spread, that the health of souls be cared for and that barbarous nations be overthrown and brought to the faith itself.*
>
> –Pope Alexander VI, Inter Caetera (1493)

I don't know why the Pope's calling Indigenous tribes "barbarous nations" when he's the one who doesn't understand that you're not supposed to wear white after Labor Day, but I digress.

Inter Caetera came to be known as the "Doctrine of Discovery," which gave full permission for European nations to rape and murder Indigenous peoples and take our stuff for like five hundred years. By giving these rights to "Christian nations," the Pope made it established canon that Indigenous peoples were, legally speaking, less than human. If you're a colonizer, you could do whatever cruel stuff you wanted to us and the church wouldn't just look the other way, they'd celebrate you as a hero.

All of this stuff is connected. Inter Caetera was written in 1493, the year Columbus returned from his 1492 expedition to ~~India~~ the Americas. Giving Spain the rights to all the land Columbus "discovered" led to the Spanish conquistador expeditions of the sixteenth and seventeenth centuries. This not only caused Galvarino's murderous knife-armed rage, but it also led to the deaths of an estimated **56 million Indigenous people** in that hundred-year period.

The Spaniards killed so many Indigenous people in the name of "exploration" that century that, according to a recent study from University College London, it cooled the Earth. This was a major cause of the Little Ice Age, where from the sixteenth to the nineteenth century the Earth's temperature dropped several degrees. One more time because it's insane: **Spanish colonizers killed so many Indigenous folks in the sixteenth century that it literally made the Earth colder!**

He might have in the Legends books. I haven't read those.

If Columbus is the Darth Vader of colonization, the Pope is his Emperor Palpatine. The difference is that the Pope doesn't have lightning powers and Darth Vader probably never had sex with a manatee.

This is all horrific, but the Doctrine of Discovery didn't stop there. It was used centuries later to justify the European colonization of Australia, Canada, and New Zealand. It even became legal precedent in the United States in the 1823 Supreme Court case *Johnson v. McIntosh*. This established that the United States government gained ownership over any land it "discovered," and that right usurped the rights of any Native folks on those lands.

And this isn't some old-timey problem; it was used as recently as 2005 in the Supreme Court case *City of Sherrill v. Oneida Indian Nation of New York*, in which the Oneida Nation tried to establish tribal sovereignty over their traditional lands that they'd purchased back. The Oneida Indian Nation lost that case, and Justice Ruth Bader Ginsberg wrote this in her majority opinion.

> Fee title to the lands occupied by Indians when the colonists arrived became vested in the sovereign—first the discovering European nation and later the original States and the United States . . .

–Justice Ruth Bader Ginsberg
City of Sherrill v. Oneida Indian Nation of New York, Majority Opinion (2005)

If you've ever heard Native folks trash talk old Notorious RBG, her using the Doctrine of Discovery in a Supreme Court ruling in 2005 is one of the main reasons!

After pressure and conversations with Indigenous leaders, Pope Francis finally rescinded the Doctrine of Discovery in 2023, over five hundred years after it was first decreed. Although it's of course nice of the Pope to come out against the Doctrine, it would have been a little more helpful if the church didn't wait five hundred years to do it.

Is that enough for the Pope to get invited to the powwow? No!

With estimated assets valued at around a trillion dollars, the Catholic Church is insanely rich. They own an estimated 177 million acres of land, which if you put it all together would be around the size of France. The Vatican storerooms contain thousands of, let's just say, "questionably attained" Indigenous artifacts, and many of these artifacts are on display in the Vatican's museums.

It doesn't take Sherlock Holmes to deduce that, during the five hundred years in which colonizers stole the land, valuables, and lives of Indigenous people in the name of Catholicism and on behalf of the Catholic Church, maybe some of their massive wealth was directly taken from those Indigenous peoples. If that's true, then maybe as part of their apology the Pope could give some of that stuff back?

If that sounds too hard, then I don't know. Maybe give every Indigenous person their own popemobile and we'll forget about everything that happened from 1493 to 1878.

If there's one thing that could help heal Indigenous trauma, it's giving all of us silly little cars.

If you're wondering why I'm stopping there, after 1878 things got a lot darker.

THE CHAPTER ABOUT INDIAN BOARDING SCHOOLS

The murder of Indigenous people by the government is a huge part of the story of westward expansion, but as the country grew, so did their methods. If "murder" was the first level of the role-playing game skill tree of colonization, what followed was more advanced, complex, and cruel.

The attempted genocide of Native people in the United States was meant to solve what politicians in the 1800s referred to as the "Indian Problem." The government and its citizens wanted our lands and resources. They didn't know what to do about the approximately fifty million Native people who were already here and had caretaken this land for thousands of years before the *Mayflower* landed.

From the seventeenth to the nineteenth century, the United States government warred with us. Then, they tried to hunt us, putting bounties on Native people and paying bounty hunters as much as fifty dollars per "Redskin scalp." Also, it's worth noting that the practice of "scalping" was popularized by European explorers and not North American Indigenous people, but I digress.

They could have tried working with us, but that makes too much sense.

When bounties didn't work, they attacked our food supplies, hunting the buffalo, a big food source of the Plains tribes, to near extinction. Finally, they forced us onto reservations through numerous Trails of Tears.

Through all of that, we persevered. So, in 1879, they came up with an even more messed-up answer to the Indian problem: attacking our cultures and our future through the forced assimilation of our children.

In the late 1800s, Unites States Army captain and human trash bag Richard Henry Pratt coined the phrase, "Kill the Indian in him, and save the man." This was a rallying cry for his proposed "Indian Boarding School" system. With culture and community being so central to Native people, the idea was that if you removed Native children from their communities and took away their cultures, you could "kill the Indian" in them and allow them to assimilate into United States society. If you did that to enough Native kids, eventually Native peoples and the cultures that surround them would disappear.

The Indian Boarding School system was part of a broad "assimilation" policy. In the 1800s, the "Indian Wars" between the United States and tribes had already been going for hundreds of years. The population of the country was increasing every year, and there was a political desire to push United States citizens to venture west and colonize the rest of the continent. It's no coincidence that the Louisiana Purchase, the Indian Removal Act, and the concept of "Manifest Destiny" all happened within a few decades of each other, and the only things standing in the way of all of that #progress were millions of Native people.

Pratt founded the first Indian boarding school in Carlisle, Pennsylvania. After his success, the government quickly funded the opening of boarding schools across the country based on Pratt's plans for Indian assimilation. Because this was the 1800s, "saving" a man had one path, and that path traveled through—you guessed it—the Catholic Church.

Though these schools were paid for through the Civilization Fund Act of 1819, they were largely run by Catholic priests hell-bent on replacing any Indigenous cultural beliefs with a love for Jesus. Native families had no choice in whether their kids attended these schools. The kids were either taken by gunpoint or, in some cases, straight-up kidnapped—ripped off the roads of their reservations by government agents who didn't inform the worried families of the whereabouts of their missing children.

If Native folks fought these abductions, the consequences were harsh, with reservations being deprived of needed supplies the government was obligated to give through treaties. In 1895, nineteen members of the Hopi Tribe of Arizona were sent to Alcatraz, where they were imprisoned for a year for resisting the government kidnapping of their children.

At the boarding schools, Native kids as young as four were restrained as their traditional long hair was cut off. They were forced to learn English and indoctrinated into the Catholic faith. Any kids who spoke their tribal languages or practiced their cultures in any way were beaten. Robbing Native kids of their traditional languages wasn't only an assimilation tactic. It also prevented kids from the same tribe from communicating with each other. Having a shared language is an important part of having in-jokes and making each other laugh, and these young kids couldn't even do that. It's one of many ways these schools were completely joyless, but it gets worse. Many kids suffered extreme physical and sexual abuse at the hands of the people who ran those schools.

The abuse was so extreme that thousands of Native kids lost their lives, many buried in unmarked graves on the school grounds. These deaths were hardly ever reported. The priests, nuns, and employees who murdered these kids through severe punishment or extreme neglect rarely faced any consequences. Though the official estimate is that around 3,100 Native kids were killed while attending the schools, it's suspected that the actual number is much higher. To this day, the remains of Native children are still being discovered on these schools' former grounds.

Indian boarding schools weren't short-lived. Carlisle Indian School opened in 1879, and the last Indian boarding school closed in 1978. When the first *Star Wars* movie came out in 1977, many of these schools were still freely abusing Native children.

If you weren't alive in 1978, know that there are Native folks your parents' or grandparents' age who are survivors of the Indian Boarding School system. And these schools were everywhere. In total, there were 526 institutions across thirty-seven states. These schools hit close to home for me. The burned-out remains of Tulalip Boarding School were right across the street from the elementary school I attended as a kid.

Tulalip Boarding School was operational on the Tulalip rez in Washington from 1905 to 1932. Though the school had closed sixty years prior to my time as a student at the tribal-run Tulalip Elementary, my class was brought to the ruins of the school for a field trip. A Tulalip elder running the trip wept and played hand drum songs as she told us of the atrocities that happened there because even at a young age, it's important we learned the truth.

The scars from these schools and this forced assimilation run deep. The trauma from these programs is still felt within Indian Country. Since this policy was so widespread, and it only ended a few decades ago, many Native folks still have survivors of these schools in our communities.

In 2024, I was invited to Pennsylvania to tour the old Carlisle Indian School. While there, I learned that a member of my tribe had been forced to attend decades earlier—a boarding school all the way across the country from our Pacific Northwest Cowlitz homelands. It was a common practice to send Native kids to schools far from their traditional territories to further alienate them from their tribal communities and cultures.

Walking through the cemetery, filled with the remains of students who tragically passed on the school's grounds, I tried to stop at each headstone and process the tragedies that happened to each kid, but I couldn't. Not because I didn't want to, but because these graves have next to no information on them. In many cases, the markers featured just the word "unknown," or the slur "Eskimo," or the name of a tribe spelled incorrectly. It shows how little these kids were valued. Even in death, there was no effort by the people who ran the school to memorialize the young lives lost there.

Carlisle is an Army town, featuring one of the United States' oldest active military bases. The first president of the United States, George Washington, even attended church services there. This is a region that loves its history, and a point of pride for Carlisle is that from the 1960s to the 1990s, the NFL team the Washington R-Skins ran their training camps within the city limits at Dickinson College.

If you ask the locals in Carlisle about the area's history, they'll glowingly talk about the town's connection to one of the National Football League's most storied franchises, named after a slur used to describe our bloody scalps, cut from our murdered bodies by settlers and turned in for bounties, paid by state governments wanting us executed just for living.

Many of the Carlisle locals aren't at all aware of the town's dark past when it comes to the treatment of actual Natives. There are professors at Dickinson doing the good work to preserve this history, and I sincerely hope the university supports them for years to come.

Indian boarding schools aren't just an American concept. Canada had its own "Indian Residential School" system, patterned after Pratt's assimilation plan, but for Canada's Indigenous First Nations population. From Africa's Mission schools and Soviet Russia's boarding schools for Siberian children to Japanese boarding schools for Ainu and Australia's Stolen Generation, to name a few examples, colonizers often target the children of Indigenous populations. Even across borders, our peoples' trauma is connected.

For a long time, Indian boarding schools were rarely talked about in your standard K-12 curriculum, with historians avoiding the subject and most Canadian and American people left completely in the dark about our countries' horrible pasts.

In the early 2020s, Canada began to come to terms with its own residential school history when 215 unmarked graves of Indigenous kids were discovered at Kamloops Indian Residential School in British

Columbia. This horrific discovery shined a spotlight on the cruelty of these schools. Pope Francis personally visited Alberta in 2022, where he apologized to the Indigenous peoples of Canada for the Catholic Church's part in this attempted genocide. The experience was a big factor in him rescinding the five-hundred-year-old Doctrine of Discovery in 2023.

In the United States, Secretary of the Interior Deb Haaland started the Federal Indian Boarding School Initiative in 2021 to document the horrific past of these schools and to identify the remains of the Native kids buried on those grounds. In 2024, former President Biden formally apologized for the United States' funding of the program. An apology doesn't bring our peoples or cultures back, nor does it undo our trauma, but it's a start.

When I talk about the genocide of Indigenous peoples, it's important to me to use the word "attempted," because despite powerful countries and organized religions spending hundreds of years trying to erase us, we're still here.

BECAUSE THE PAST TWO CHAPTERS WERE PRETTY HEAVY, HERE'S A PICTURE OF CHEROKEE ACTIVIST AND LEADER WILMA MANKILLER KICKING GENERAL PRATT IN THE NUTS!

INDIGENOUS EXCELLENCE #3

Deb Haaland

Deb Haaland, or "Auntie Deb" if you're young, hip, and Native, is a total badass. A "Thirty-Fifth Generation New Mexican" and an enrolled member of the Laguna Pueblo tribe, Haaland went from raising a daughter as a single mother in poverty in her twenties to, decades later, becoming the first Native American to ever be appointed to a secretary-level position in a United States presidential cabinet. Also, she's on government record as someone who makes a mean green chile chicken stew.

Haaland has held a ton of titles in her life: poet, counselor, casino manager, and chairwoman are a few of many. She dove into politics in New Mexico in the late 2000s and, along with Sharice Davids, was among the first Native women ever elected to United States Congress. Deb was racking up historic accomplishments like Kyrie Irving hitting three-pointers, but they don't get much more historic than in 2021 when Auntie Deb was named secretary of the interior by President Biden.

Aside from the amazing representation win for Native folks in national politics, this appointment was historic for a TON of other reasons. The Department of the Interior is the department of the United States Government that covers federal lands and natural resources. They also run the Bureau of Indian Affairs, which is a wide-reaching organization managing most aspects of Indian Country, from reservation lands to protecting treaty rights and everything in between. Anything touching the government's obligation to tribes probably goes through the BIA. For hundreds of years, non-Natives ran this department. With Haaland's appointment, it was the FIRST time a Native person had final say over the government's direction when it came to Native issues.

> *This moment is profound when we consider the fact that a former secretary of the interior once proclaimed his goal to "civilize or exterminate" us. I'm a living testament to the failure of that horrific ideology.*
>
> –Deb Haaland (2020)
> Speech accepting her secretary of the interior nomination

Upon her appointment, Haaland flew in like a matriarch on a mission, creating programs to tackle long-standing issues in Indian Country that had for centuries been ignored by the BIA—issues like investigating the Missing and Murdered Indigenous People epidemic, renaming federal lands to remove straight-up slurs against Natives, and establishing the Federal Indian Boarding

School Initiative to document the crimes and trauma caused by Indian boarding schools.

Many of Haaland's family members were survivors of the Indian Boarding School system. Those schools were under the purview of the secretary of the interior. That Haaland was able, decades later, to use a department that had caused so much harm in our communities to bring real healing to survivors of that horrible system is so awesome.

And the expectations for Haaland were sky-high. Natives and non-Natives expected her to fix centuries of government-caused problems in Indian Country in a Thanos-level finger snap. Though that would be impossible without a silver bracelet full of Infinity Stones, what she was able to pull off in her handful of years in that office is inspiring.

Haaland's body of work is a testament to the idea that through determination and resilience, Native people can accomplish anything. The best part is, Haaland is still active as a political force, kicking ass and taking names for the people of New Mexico. She's also inspiring the next generation of Native people to run for public office. I hope that her example leads to more Native representation in government as a whole. Haaland has set such a great example, showing that Native people being in charge, or at least having a say in what happens in our lands, can bring about some great things.

As a perfect visual depiction of her Indigenous excellence, enjoy a full-page drawing of her kicking Christopher Columbus in the nuts.

This drawing of Deb Haaland
kicking Christopher Columbus in the nuts
is my best work!

SECTION FOUR

AP TRIBAL COUNCIL MEMBER

You've learned the remedial stuff, got the basics down, and fancy-danced your way through advanced. Now, it's time to learn about big things like the Land Back movement, the modern struggles of Indigenous people, and what the Pilgrims smelled like when they landed at Plymouth Rock!

GUIDE FOR HOLLYWOOD

Here is a list of emotions Native people are capable of that aren't just "stoic"

Oftentimes, when Native characters appear in television and film, we are portrayed only as stoic warriors and wise medicine men and women. Our faces are usually stuck in an emotionless expression as we stare at the wind while flutes play and we think about our sacred ways.

Here are some lesser-known emotions that Native people ALSO feel!

Letting an elder cut in front of you at dinner

Watching the same elder hog the microphone at a tribal council meeting

Snaggable

Tradish

Lost the beadwork drop

Won the beadwork drop

Looking at Wes Studi

Being Wes Studi

QUIZ: WHAT DID THE PILGRIMS SMELL LIKE WHEN THEY LANDED AT PLYMOUTH ROCK?

They smelled like shit. Seriously. When the Wampanoag people greeted the pilgrims, there are A LOT of historical accounts from the 1700s Natives talking about how rank those European dorks were.

You might be thinking, "Of course the Pilgrims smelled bad, they were on a boat for two months!" But the thing is, they smelled terrible BEFORE that! Hygiene in Europe was truly awful at the time, with basically everybody except for the super royalty going their entire lives without even taking ONE bath. The Natives, on the other hand, would regularly bathe in rivers and streams and smelled GREAT.

Patuxet tribal member Tisquantum, who lived in and around what is now called Massachusetts, even tried to teach the pilgrims how to bathe, but they REFUSED to learn. They say the pilgrims "discovered" America, but it'd be nice if on the way they discovered a bar of soap.

PLEASE GIVE US OUR LAND BACK

The modern #LandBack movement

If you've interacted with a group of Native folks within the past ten years, first off, congrats for being an ally! Secondly, you've probably seen or heard the term "Land Back" or "#LandBack," but what does Land Back actually mean?

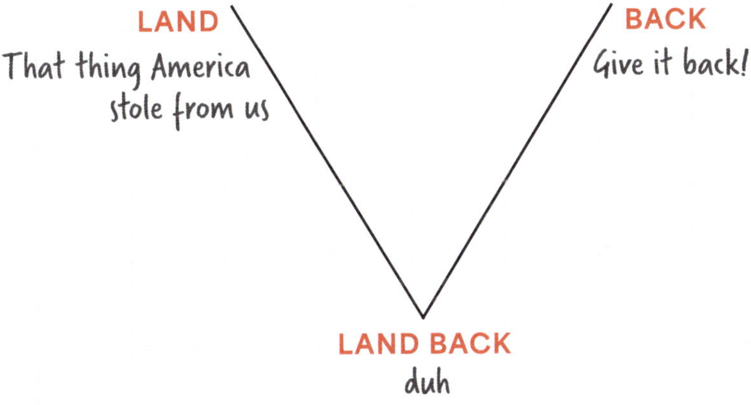

Now, before you get defensive, it doesn't mean Natives kicking non-Natives out of their houses and pushing them onto boats to ship them back to wherever they came from. Well, for some Natives it does, but the vast majority of us aren't that aggro. There are two ways to look at Land Back, or the "Land Back movement":

As a philosophy: Though the idea of returning the land to Indigenous peoples has been around since colonizers started colonizing, the movement was popularized in the late 2010s. It was coined by a sacred viral Instagram post from Blackfoot tribal member and content creator Arnell Tailfeathers and amplified by nonprofit NDN Collective.

NDN Collective founder and Oglala Lakota Nation citizen Nick Tilsen says the goal of Land Back is to "get Indigenous lands back into Indigenous hands." A big thing to keep in mind is that every tribe is its own sovereign nation, and what Land Back looks like to one tribe probably isn't the same for another tribe. All Land Back fights are different, but many of these fights have these aspects in common:

1. Holding the government accountable to honor its treaty obligations—meaning, the government can't elbow a tribe aside if they want to build a railroad, pipeline, or weird ugly president mountain on that tribe's treaty-given territory.
2. Allowing tribes jurisdiction over public lands in their aboriginal territories. If there's a national park on Nez Perce land, the Nez Perce should be the park's legal caretakers.
3. Allowing tribes to write, change, and enforce their own laws democratically in their aboriginal territories. This makes our authority as sovereign nations even stronger.
4. Healing centuries of colonization of our lands and the attempted genocide of our peoples, of which Land Back is a critical first step.

And the reasons for the Land Back movement aren't just "It would be nice, and also in many cases the government is legally required to do it, please read our treaties seriously WTF is wrong with them?" It's also because tribal nations have been here for thousands of years and we know what works on our lands.

The United States is a country of "rugged individualism." The thing about individualism is, it's a worldview where it's a little bit okay to be a lotta bit selfish. That's compounded by capitalism, the economic system that the United States revolves around like a tetherball swinging around a pole made of stolen metal of the precious variety.

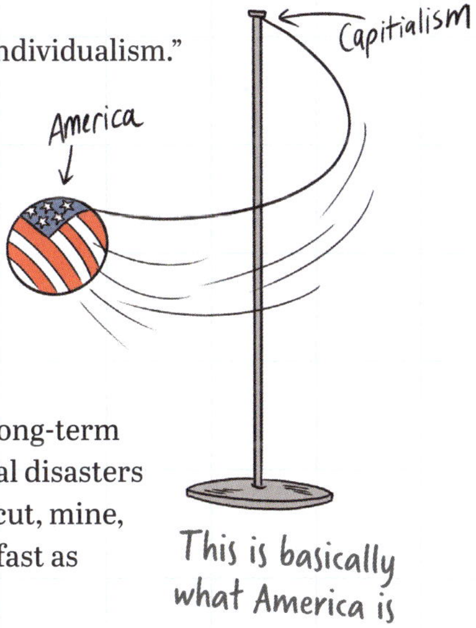

Capitalism prioritizes fast gains over any long-term planning. Our recent climate and ecological disasters are in part caused by companies trying to cut, mine, hunt, fish, and drill their way to profits as fast as possible with little concern for the future.

Traditionally, an Indigenous mindset is more focused on sustainability. The Cherokee people's "Seven Generations" principle is the idea that your choices should be made to help people seven generations in the future. A lot of Indigenous folks ascribe to this. If that sounds at all familiar, Seventh Generation is also the name of a brand of dish soap you can buy at Whole Foods, so maybe that's where you heard it?

Essentially, if Native people have been caretakers of our aboriginal territories for thousands of years, there's a chance that we might know more about our homelands than a country that's been around for barely an eyeblink. The United States being unfamiliar with our lands and just kind of making things up as they go along is a sizeable reason Florida is mostly kudzu vines and California is mostly wildfires.

And it's not only about the land. This also includes hunting and fishing practices. When the government makes blanket bans on that stuff, they rarely do it with tribal communities and our treaties in mind. Our treaties in many cases explicitly give us hunting and fishing rights, but Native people are often wrongfully punished for doing things we're legally allowed to do.

Billy Frank Jr. of the Nisqually Tribe was a famous activist and advocate for these practices. Due to commercial fishing operations affecting salmon populations in the 1900s, the Washington State government placed a blanket ban on fishing in many of their waterways. The Washington government allowed fishing corporations to take, and in some cases outright handed over, these lands and waters AND banned Natives from using them. They didn't just take away our rights; they sold those rights to the highest bidder, which sucks more than a room full of Roombas.

Frank Jr.'s tribe had fished those lands for generations, and it was even written into many local tribes' treaties that they could continue those traditions. He tested his treaty granting fishing rights and was arrested over fifty times through a series of "fish-in" protests in the 1960s and 1970s. The protests were big news, and A-list Hollywood celebrities even participated in them.

The point of these protests was to show that the government shouldn't make unilateral decisions that infringe on the sustainable hunting practices of Indigenous peoples without their say, and it worked! The Washington State government now consults with tribes when considering those kinds of decisions. Because of that partnership, and with the consultation of Indigenous leaders, salmon populations are starting to increase, helping undo a century of ecological damage caused by commercial fishing. Though this predates the modern Land Back movement, giving Indigenous peoples agency over our lands in that way is one of the many things the movement is now fighting for.

If a land acknowledgment states that Native people were the original caretakers of these lands, the Land Back movement demands that our responsibilities and authority over our lands isn't only in the past tense.

In action: Does Land Back actually happen, and if it does, what does it look like?

It DOES happen, and it looks as beautiful as a Native hand covered in turquoise rings. Here are a few of many recent Land Back wins.

- In 2025, the nonprofit Western Rivers Conservancy donated seventy-three square miles of land to the Yurok Tribe. The land, located along the Klamath River of California, is part of the Yuroks' traditional territories. They've turned part of the land into a salmon sanctuary, which will help replenish the area's salmon population. Hell yeah!
- That same year, the state of Illinois returned over a thousand acres of land, including Shabbona Lake State Park, to the Prairie Band Potawatomi Nation. This land is in the PBPN's traditional territory, and the land was returned because the United States sold the land in the 1830s despite not legally owning it. This was them attempting to fix their mistake. Governments apologizing and doing the right thing? You love to see it!
- In 2023, the Cowlitz Tribe even had our own Land Back win when Capitol Land Trust returned to us seventeen acres of land near the Cowlitz River in southern Washington State. Will we use this land to build an Ilani part two? My fingers are crossed so hard that my knuckles are cracking, and I don't even mind the pain!

Every tribe is on their own #LandBack journey, and all tribes' needs and wants are different. But the thing about these examples is, after the tribes got their lands back, nothing crazy happened! Nobody was dragged from their homes! In many cases, the tribe, environment, and local community were all better off for it. By tribes having legal claim to their aboriginal territories, these Land Back wins are helping those tribes achieve economic sovereignty too! That means they can earn money to help their people!

Ojibwe tribal member, Land Back movement advocate, and Minnesota Lieutenant Governor Peggy Flanagan summarized Land Back in this fantastic quote:

> ***Land Back isn't just a hashtag or something you see on a T-shirt or on a flag that is being flown. It is intentional, detailed, hard work that we do together.***
>
> –Lt. Governor Peggy Flanagan
> *NPR* (2024)

So if you've got any spare land laying around, maybe think about gifting it to your local tribe? It's the right thing to do; it'll genuinely help your local community. If it sweetens the deal, the tribe might give you a front row seat at their next elder's bingo night, and those are hard to get!

WHAT'LL HAPPEN TO YOU IF YOU TRY TO PET A WILD BUFFALO

A haiku

That big buffalo

Will gore you out of your jeans.

Don't pet it, dummy!

SACRED FAILS #2

Wrongful sweat lodge death lawsuits

Sweat lodges are a regular spiritual practice used in many Indigenous cultures of the Americas. Practically speaking, a sweat lodge is a hut made of natural materials: a base built from branches, covered in mud, animal hides, or blankets, with heated rocks in the center occasionally doused in water to produce steam, a little like a sauna. Spiritually, it's a purification ceremony often called a "sweat" that involves prayer and songs. It's VERY Native, but that hasn't stopped non-Native New Ager types from putting on their own "sweats" and accidentally killing a bunch of people while doing it.

Practiced for hundreds of years, if not thousands, by the Plains tribes of the Midwest before spreading across Indian Country, sweats are exactly the kind of "sacred traditions from the elders" that non-Natives love to steal and claim for themselves. The thing is, if you don't know what you're doing, sweat lodges are dangerous! It's like a dreamcatcher if the dreamcatcher could also kill you.

Non-Native New Ager types started putting on their own sweats in the 1970s, and since then, nine people died due to these "I don't know what the hell I'm doing" colonizer-ass ceremonies. That's more than double the amount of people who have died from wolf attacks in North America in that same time frame. Non-Native sweat lodges are literally more fatal to Americans than wolves! (Yikes!)

The most infamous New Ager sweat lodge death case was caused in 2009 by a "practical mysticism" teacher and dumbass named James Arthur Ray. He ran something called the "Spiritual Warrior" retreat in Arizona. It cost around ten thousand dollars to attend the week-long retreat. While there, dozens of non-Natives slept in the desert without shelter and weren't allowed to drink water for two days as part of a "vision quest" before attending a "sweat lodge" conducted by Ray. Was Ray Native? Of course not. Did Natives trained in sweat practices build the lodge? Nope! Since Ray had no real training, did he basically cram a bunch of people who hadn't drunk anything for days into an oven in the Arizona desert heat? Hell yeah he did.

After several hours in the sweat lodge/death oven, around twenty of the attendees were sent to the hospital with serious burns and injuries. Three of the attendees tragically passed away during or shortly after the sweat. Instead of helping the wounded, Ray allegedly fled the scene because he was "scared." In a conference call with the participants after the event, he reportedly brought in a "spiritual channeler." The "channeler" said they'd communicated with the people who died and, "according to the spirits," they didn't want to be alive because they'd "left their bodies in the sweat lodge" and their spirits "were having so much fun." (Double yikes!)

As you'd expect, Ray got the mysticism sued out of him to the tune of millions of dollars. For his crimes, he was sentenced to two years in prison. This is ONE example of non-Native sweats going wrong, but this kind of thing happens all the time!

Aside from the cultural appropriation and non-Natives feeling entitled to whatever aspect of Native cultures and spirituality they want, there are a ton of problems with these sweat lodges. First, conducting a traditional sweat takes years of training. Part of that is to learn the culture and traditions surrounding these ceremonies, but another part is to learn how to not accidentally kill your attendees!

This is one of the many things that burns me about non-Natives co-opting our cultures and traditions. Anyone who spends five minutes on "Spiritual TikTok" might think they know how to smudge, go on a vision quest, or put together a sweat. Whatever they're doing probably isn't the "real thing," and by participating in whatever weird version of Indigenous culture they learned about on Reddit, they're making a mockery of this specific and beautiful cultural practice many Native folks value.

Also, when Native folks talk about our cultures and traditions being passed down for hundreds of years, it's not just being said to sound "sacred" (well, okay, maybe it is a little . . .). It's being said to let you know that this practice has been harnessed, perfected, and sharpened over centuries, and all of the kinks have been worked out. In a Native ceremony run by Natives who know what they're doing, you'll be taken care of spiritually AND physically. A random New Ager influencer probably won't be able to make that same guarantee.

If after reading this, you want to do a sweat lodge, great! Make sure a Native is running it, because if it's a non-Native New Ager sweat, the chances of you dying in there are probably not low!

COOL MOMENTS IN INDIGENOUS HISTORY #4

Indigenous Hawaiians killing Captain Cook on Valentine's Day!

A lot of the stories in this book are about colonizers who committed horrific acts against Indigenous peoples and kinda sorta got away with it. Captain James Cook isn't one of those stories. He gets absolutely wrecked by Indigenous Hawaiians, and it rocks.

Cook's résumé as an "explorer" is extensive. Born in England in 1728, he was the first recorded European to sail the Hawaiian Islands and the east coast of Australia and the first to map New Zealand's coastline. When it comes to European explorers of the 1700s, he was basically the Larry Bird of "discovering" lands in the Pacific for the British Crown.

He and his crew of sailors were also infamous hotheads. When mapping New Zealand, they killed several Māori people over small misunderstandings, burned down an entire village on the island of Mo'orea (in what is now French Polynesia) over a missing goat, and spread a ton of diseases everywhere they visited. That last one doesn't have anything to do with having a temper, it's just gross.

In 1778, Cook and his men "discovered" Hawaii, and at the start, the experience went great for them. Their boat landed on Hawaii's main island during a harvest festival. Cook's men were greeted with gifts by the Indigenous Hawaiians, but Cook ruined the vibes when he tried to kidnap Hawaii's supreme monarch Kalaniʻōpuʻu over a stolen rowboat.

Not letting that stand, the Indigenous Hawaiians attacked Cook's boat, killing him, ripping his body to shreds, burning it, and gifting the pieces to the area's chiefs (hell yeah). To put a rose on this beautiful story, Cook was killed on the 14th of February: Valentine's Day. How romantic!

FLOWCHART: IF YOU'RE A MISSIONARY, WHAT WILL HAPPEN IF YOU VISIT THE SENTINELESE TRIBE OF INDIA?

You're not supposed to visit the Sentinelese people of India's North Sentinel Island. Living on an island over seven hundred miles from the Indian mainland, the Sentinelese are considered "the most isolated people in the world." As an "uncontacted" tribe, they haven't been touched by colonization or any form of technology aside from their own traditions. Wanting to preserve their culture and keep them safe, the Indian government made it a jailable offense to visit the island and even set up a buffer zone that is constantly patrolled to keep boaters away!

Who would be dumb enough to try to visit this protected island? Missionaries trying to convert the Sentinelese to Christianity, of course! This happened most recently in 2018. The Sentinelese are known for being aggressive, and it didn't end well for the missionary. In this simple flowchart, we explain what'll happen if you visit North Sentinel Island!

THESE PEOPLE AREN'T INVITED TO THE POWWOW #4

John Wayne

John Wayne, "The Duke," the king of the Western film, one of the most romanticized actors in film history, and a man who is FOR SURE not invited to the powwow. Wayne is known for his tough cowboy roles, his personification of the American Old West mythos, and a ton of movies where he heroically shoots 1800s Indian "Savage" stereotypes in the back.

The characters he played in his films hated Natives, but would you believe that he wasn't the coolest dude in real life either? (Shocker!)

John Wayne (real name Marion Morrison, which makes a ton of sense) was an infamous bigot, McCarthyism supporter, and draft dodger. During World War II, many big-time Hollywood actors and musicians served in the United States military, but old Marion Wayne kept getting draft deferments. He used his film career as an excuse not to fight for the country he claimed to love. John Ford, director of Wayne vehicle *The Searchers,* was so pissed off about Wayne's draft dodging that he kept cussing him out over it on the set of one of his films until actor Robert Montgomery intervened to prevent a fistfight from breaking out.

One of the reasons he was so good at hating Natives onscreen is that he hated Native people in real life too! When, at the 1973 Academy Awards, actress Sacheen Littlefeather declined Marlon Brando's Best

Actor award for his role in *The Godfather*, she read a speech prepared by Brando about the mistreatment of Native people. In response, John Wayne reportedly had to be restrained from jumping onstage and physically attacking her. He wasn't willing to fight Nazis, but he was allegedly more than happy to fight a woman talking about Native rights. What a guy!

His hatred of Native people wasn't a one-time thing. In a 1971 interview with *Playboy* magazine, he had this to say:

> I don't feel we did wrong in taking this great country away from them, if that's what you're asking. Our so-called stealing of this country from them was just a matter of survival. There were great numbers of people who needed new land, and the Indians were selfishly trying to keep it for themselves.
>
> –John Wayne
> *Playboy* (1971)

This answer is WILD, but what's even wilder is that the reporter's question was "American Indians have played an important—if subordinate—role in your Westerns. Do you feel any empathy with them?"

I mean, come on. This wasn't a hard-hitting interview with Edward R. Murrow, this was a feature in *Playboy* magazine, most known for giving pre-internet folks access to pictures of naked butts. It was an easy softball designed to make him look good, and his response was to call Natives "selfish" for "trying to keep [the land] for themselves." Dude, what's your problem?

In the same interview, he also said, "I don't see why we owe them [Indians] anything" because the mistreatment of Native people was "so far back." Keep in mind this was 1971, when Native people were still actively being sent to jail for practicing our cultures and Native kids were still being kidnapped by the government and forced to attend boarding schools.

Killing Natives onscreen was a huge part of this guy's career, and it seems like he despised us in real life. If we're "selfish" for not sharing our land, then I guess we're also selfish for not sharing our delicious blue corn muffins, because John Wayne, you are not invited to the powwow!

INDIGENOUS EXCELLENCE #4

Lily Gladstone

In over one hundred years of film, Native actors have rarely been allowed to play more than sacred medicine people, stoic warriors, or a superhero whose power is that they can grow taller. We rarely are given prestigious roles that would put us up for any real awards or recognition.

In the "Best Actress" category, there is only one Native actor to win a Golden Globe and Screen Actors Guild Award and receive an Oscar nomination, and those accomplishments happened within the past few years! Her name is Lily Gladstone, and she freaking rocks.

Gladstone is a member of the Blackfeet Nation of Montana who rose to prominence playing the role of Mollie Burkhart in the critically acclaimed Martin Scorsese film *Killers of the Flower Moon*. She continued to smash it out of the park in films like *Fancy Dance*, *The Wedding Banquet*, and many others. Prior to her ascent into the spotlight, she worked for years in independent film and theater.

One of the things that is so impressive about Lily's rise is that, for decades, there wasn't a talent pipeline between Indian Country and Hollywood. Native actors were doing fantastic work all across the country, but big-name agents, producers, and directors rarely visited Native-focused theater companies like Native Voices in Los Angeles or Red Eagle Soaring in Seattle, where Lily developed her craft. Lily was so undeniably fantastic that not only did she rise to the top, but she's helping set an example for how Hollywood can build a new talent pipeline. She's proven that there are fantastic Native actors doing great work everywhere, not just in the major acting hubs of New York, Los Angeles, and Chicago. Lily isn't only succeeding for herself; she's using her platform to lift up other Native creatives, artists, and causes in fantastic ways.

Lily often guests on small Native-hosted podcasts and shouts out Native creatives by name, from giving shine to Cherokee Nation comedian and writer Shea Vassar in interviews, to having the luxury fashion brand Gucci collaborate with Indigenous artist Joe Big Mountain on her Academy Awards dress. She even uses her powerful name to give credibility and a spotlight to other Native-directed films, like the documentaries *Sugarcane* and *Bring Them Home*. While receiving awards for her role in *Killers of the Flower Moon*, Gladstone spent many of her *Killers* acceptance speeches advocating for the smaller indie film *Fancy Dance*, directed by Seneca–Cayuga filmmaker Erica Tremblay, to receive a distribution deal, which it later received through Apple TV.

Being the "first" to do anything is a ton of pressure, and especially for Indian Country, what little representation we have in media is put under an extremely harsh microscope. There's often an expectation that a Native artist needs to represent everyone with absolute perfection. It's an impossible task that Lily handles with grace, humor, and Indigenous badassery. I mean, look at this quote from the speech she gave at the Golden Globes after winning an award for her role in *Killers of the Flower Moon*:

> This is an historic win. . . . This is for every rez kid, every little urban kid, every little Native kid out there who has a dream.
>
> –Lily Gladstone
> Golden Globes (2024)

She opened her Golden Globes speech by speaking in her Blackfeet language. Less than fifty years before she gave this speech, openly celebrating Native culture like that could have gotten Lily thrown in jail. To go from that to where we are today is incredible.

Though I can't give Lily Gladstone an Oscar, I'd like to give her my highest honor: this doodle of John Wayne getting kicked in the nuts by a buffalo, because John Wayne was a bad actor who probably smelled like bourbon, and Lily Gladstone is truly great.

YOU'RE WELCOME #3

American Democracy

A lot of people refer to the US of A as "the greatest country in the world." One of the big reasons they give when saying this is our homegrown American democracy, a government by the people and for the people. When the Founding Fathers of the United States wanted to create this system of government to replace monarchies, they used their combined genius to craft it through sheer smarts and patriotism—JUST KIDDING!

They stole everything from the Haudenosaunee Confederacy, a group of tribes in North America who had been practicing this style of government for hundreds of years before European contact!

Founded around the twelfth century AD, the Haudenosaunee Confederacy was a collection of five tribes: the Mohawk, Oneida, Onondaga, Cayuga, and Seneca. They're all based around what is now the Northeastern United States and the southeast of Canada. They were later joined by the Tuscarora to create the Six Nations Confederacy that is still active today.

The Confederacy is governed by a system that is pretty dang similar to American democracy. They had their own constitution, "The Great Law of Peace." Much like Congress, each tribe had ten chiefs who reported to the Confederacy's "Grand Council" on behalf of their constituents. Agreements between tribes were even recorded on "wampum belts," much like the parchments used to record United States law.

One difference between America and the Confederacy is that the Confederacy was led matrilineally. Women (known as "clan mothers") had final say over most decisions. If the Founding Fathers also stole that one, maybe we'd be better off as a country? Just saying!

These hearts are for the clan mothers.

There are similarities between the Haudenosaunee Confederacy and American democracy, but does that really mean the Founding Fathers stole it from Native people? Oh, it for sure does!

The Founding Fathers were all born and raised in a system of government that reported to the English monarchy. Being ruled by kings and queens is all they knew! Once they decided to split from the British like Beyoncé leaving Destiny's Child, they had to invent a new system from scratch. Of course they looked around to see what the other groups around them were doing. Founding father and electric kite lover Benjamin Franklin said as much in a letter he wrote in 1751:

> *It would be a very strange Thing, if six Nations of ignorant Savages should be capable of forming a Scheme for such an Union, and be able to execute it in such a Manner, as that it has subsisted Ages, and appears indissoluble; and yet that a like Union should be impracticable for ten or a Dozen English Colonies, to whom it is more necessary, and must be more advantageous; and who cannot be supposed to want an equal Understanding of their Interests.*

–Benjamin Franklin
to James Parker (1751)

Wow, way to give the Haudenosaunee Confederacy the most back-handed compliment possible, Ben.

Though Franklin played a hand in the creation of the American system of government, there were a ton of Founding Fathers, so it's not for me to say that they were all inspired by the Haudenosaunee Confederacy. Good thing I don't need to say it, because they said it themselves!

John Adams, the second president of the United States, who many call the "Architect of American Government," complimented tribal governments many times in his formative writings, "The Defense of the Constitutions."

In 1785, James Monroe and James Madison even met with a Haudenosaunee Chief to learn how the Confederacy's government was structured. Madison incorporated those lessons into the Federalist Papers, a VERY influential document in crafting the United States Constitution.

Not only did the Founding Fathers love stealing Native land, they also loved stealing Native governmental structures! Next time someone tells you that United States democracy is the best political system in the world, don't be surprised if a member of one of the Six Nations says, "You're welcome."

"You're Welcome" for every Nation!

INDIAN NAME GENERATOR

In the introduction to this book, I mentioned that reading it would not give you an Indian name. I said that to discourage people who aren't interested in doing the work. You, on the other hand, are different. You earned this.

Here is your 100% sacred Indian Name Generator.

FIRST LETTER OF YOUR FIRST NAME

A:	Wes	N:	Wes
B:	Wes	O:	Wes
C:	Wes	P:	Wes
D:	Wes	Q:	Wes
E:	Wes	R:	Wes
F:	Wes	S:	Wes
G:	Wes	T:	Wes
H:	Wes	U:	Wes
I:	Wes	V:	Wes
J:	Wes	W:	Wes
K:	Wes	X:	Wes
L:	Wes	Y:	Wes
M:	Wes	Z:	Wes

FIRST LETTER OF YOUR LAST NAME

A:	Studi	N:	Studi
B:	Studi	O:	Studi
C:	Studi	P:	Studi
D:	Studi	Q:	Studi
E:	Studi	R:	Studi
F:	Studi	S:	Studi
G:	Studi	T:	Studi
H:	Studi	U:	Studi
I:	Studi	V:	Studi
J:	Studi	W:	Studi
K:	Studi	X:	Studi
L:	Studi	Y:	Studi
M:	Studi	Z:	Studi

May your new Indian name lead you to a successful acting career and a role in the hilarious 1999 superhero comedy *Mystery Men*. Aho!

TIMELINE: THE ATTEMPTED GENOCIDE OF NATIVE PEOPLE IS WAY, WAY, WAY MORE RECENT THAN YOU THINK!

The government's systemic mistreatment of Native people didn't stop at the Wounded Knee Massacre of 1890. Way too much stuff happened after that too! Here are a few (of many) good and bad historic moments between the United States government and Natives over the past one hundred-ish years, juxtaposed with other historic moments that happened around that time.

1890: The first powered airplane took flight in France, and the United States cavalry murdered over one hundred Native folks (mostly unarmed women and children) in an event called the "Wounded Knee Massacre."

1893: The Chicago World's 'Fair brought futuristic technology to the Windy City. That same year, United States-backed forces overthrew Queen Lili'uokalani of Hawaii, instilling a puppet government called the Republic of Hawaii as a pathway to the United States annexing the territory and officially making it part of the US later that decade.

1921: Cheez-It crackers were sold in stores for the first time, and the Osage Reign of Terror began. This is an event where hundreds of Osage were systemically murdered in Oklahoma by their non-Native neighbors looking to steal the Osage people's oil rights. These events were later dramatized in the film *Killers of the Flower Moon*.

1924: The first-ever Macy's Thanksgiving Day Parade took place, and the Indian Citizenship Act of 1924 was signed into law, finally making Native people United States citizens.

1953: The classic Disney animated film *Peter Pan* was released, and House Concurrent Resolution 108 was adopted by the United States Congress. This resolution was intended to revoke federal recognition status from, and the government's responsibility to, all Native people. In total, around one hundred tribes lost their federal recognition because of this resolution.

This was one of a long line of bills in the 1940s and 1950s that were a part of the United States government's "termination policy" for tribes. Essentially, the government wanted to stop paying its treaty obligations, so they disestablished as many tribes as possible. The public reason was to integrate Indians into civilized society, but the real reason was to cut costs and steal our reservation land, because of course it was!

1934: The first *Flash Gordon* comic hit the presses, and the Indian Reorganization Act was signed into law. This act allowed Native people to start businesses on tribal lands and improved our tribal sovereignty.

1962: The Beatles released their first album, and Native people finally received the right to vote in all fifty states. Though the Indian Citizenship Act of 1924 formally gave Native people the right to vote, it took several decades for all fifty states to actually let us vote, with the state of Utah being the final holdout. Thanks, Utah!

1953

1968

1934

1962

1968: The Apollo 8 mission launched, becoming the first time that humans ever orbited the moon, and the Indian Civil Rights Act was signed into law. Prior to 1968, Native people didn't have many of the protections given to United States citizens in the Bill of Rights, and this gave Native people things like the right to free speech, right to a trial by jury, and a lot of other rights that Natives were denied for centuries.

Also in 1968: McDonald's officially launched the Big Mac nationwide, and the American Indian Movement (AIM) formed, becoming a major player in the Indian Civil Rights Movement. Delicious!

1970: The Jackson 5 released their megahit song "I'll Be There," and President Nixon formally condemned the United States termination policy toward Native tribes. This ended that nearly two-decade long policy and instead shifted to "self-determination," putting tribes in control of their own destinies. The new (and way better!) policy was signed into law with the Indian Self-Determination and Education Assistance Act of 1975.

1973: The Miami Dolphins finish the first and only completely undefeated season in NFL history, and hundreds of members of the Oglala Lakota Tribe, in partnership with the American Indian Movement, occupied the site of the 1890 Wounded Knee Massacre in South Dakota. During the seventy-one-day standoff, two Sioux men were killed by federal agents and many more were wounded.

Also in 1970: The Family Planning Services and Population Research Act of 1970 was signed into law. Though this act was intended for "family planning," it was actually used as justification for the forced sterilization of Native women.

Native women of childbearing age were targeted by healthcare workers and coerced–and in some instances, forced–to become sterilized. In the half decade this policy was active, at least 25% of Native women of childbearing age were sterilized. It was such a crisis that it was even reported to the United Nations as a government-funded modern form of genocide. If you wanted yet another reason why some Native people have trust issues with the federal government, this is one point in a list so long, it could stretch to the sun.

1973

1969

1970

1969: Neil Armstrong became the first human to set foot on the moon, and the United Indians of All Tribes used the Fort Laramie Treaty to claim ownership over Alcatraz Penitentiary. Hundreds of Natives occupied Alcatraz Island in California's Bay Area until US Marshals kicked them out in 1971.

1975: The Vietnam War ended, and the Pine Ridge Shootout occurred on the Pine Ridge reservation in South Dakota. The shootout, between members of the American Indian Movement and the FBI, left two FBI agents dead. Two years later in 1977, Turtle Mountain Band of Chippewa Indians member and prominent AIM organizer Leonard Peltier was sentenced to two life sentences for first degree murder for the killings.

1978: The world saw the release of the first *Garfield* comic strip , and the American Indian Movement disbanded after the government worked to infiltrate the organization and many of its leaders were arrested. No, I'm not implying that Garfield disbanded AIM, but can you imagine?!

Also in 1978: Prominent AIM organizers Dennis Banks and Russell Means lead the "Longest Walk," a several-thousand-mile march from Sacramento to Washington, DC, to protest anti-tribal sovereignty legislation.

Thousands of people joined the roughly five-month-long march. It was so successful that not only did it convince politicians to vote those pieces of legislation down, it also lead to the American Indian Religious Freedom Act and the Indian Child Welfare Act being signed into law. AIRA finally made it legal for Native people to practice our traditional cultures and speak our tribal languages without fear of arrest or punishment from the federal government. ICWA ended the near century-long policy of forcing Native kids to attend Indian boarding schools.

These are huge wins for Native rights, and that they only happened a few decades ago is nuts.

1975

1978

1988

This conviction was controversial for many reasons. Mainly, there wasn't much proof that Peltier killed either FBI agent, much of the evidence used in the case was found to be fabricated by the FBI, and witnesses were pressured to implicate Peltier in the crime. This was seen by a lot of people as a politically motivated sentencing to throw the book at an AIM leader and destroy the larger Native rights movement. Despite public backlash for Peltier's arrest, he remained in prison for fifty years.

1988: Classic video game *Super Mario Bros. 3* was released in Japan, and the United States signed the Indian Gaming Regulatory Act into law. This was a watershed moment in allowing tribes to run casinos on reservation and trust lands. With "Indian casinos" being a touchpoint for how non-Natives view Native cultures, it's wild how these casinos are still new as a concept. Heck, my tribe's casino didn't open until 2017!

2016: Justin Timberlake's "Can't Stop the Feeling" topped the Billboard charts the same year the Standing Rock Water Protectors protested the building of the Dakota Access Oil Pipeline through the Standing Rock Sioux Reservation of North Dakota.

These actions, where the government violated their treaty obligations by approving the construction of an illegal oil pipeline through Standing Rock Sioux territory, were a rallying call for Native activists. The hashtag #NODAPL trended across social media, including videos of the National Guard and riot police attacking tribal members and allies with rubber bullets, pepper spray, and water hoses in below-freezing conditions. They were punished just for protesting on their own lands, which they had legal title to.

The protestors' actions became an international news story. We owe the media's greater awareness of Native people and modern Native issues on these protest actions and the extensive media attention they received.

2000: The PlayStation 2 launched, and the Cowlitz Indian Tribe finally, after 150 years of fighting, received federal recognition. This is a big deal to me, so I'm including it on this list, and there's nothing you can do to stop me!

2000

2016

2020

2020: The COVID-19 pandemic grinded the world to a standstill the same year Savanna's Act was signed into law. This act addresses the Missing and Murdered Indigenous Women, Girls, and Two-Spirit People (MMIWG2S) epidemic that has affected Indian Country for years.

Indigenous women are more than twice as likely as white women to be victims of violence in their lifetimes, with the majority of those crimes being perpetrated by non-Native men. Additionally, around 85% of our two-spirit kin and 82% of Indigenous men experience violence at some point in their lives. For years, loopholes and government apathy had prevented these cases from being investigated or prosecuted. The federal government has finally started allocating the resources necessary to start solving and preventing these horrific crimes.

2021: *Reservation Dogs* and *Rutherford Falls*, the first two Native-created television shows in United States history, debuted the same year Deb Haaland was appointed secretary of the interior. Haaland was the first Native person appointed to a presidential cabinet in United States history, and she rocks. Love you, Auntie Deb!

Also in 2021: The governor of Colorado finally rescinded an 1864 law making it legal to kill Native people in the state. That's right, they JUST took this law off the books!

2022: Will Smith slapped Chris Rock at the Academy Awards the same year a hotel in South Dakota made the news for banning all Native people from stepping foot on their property or patronizing any of their businesses. This SUCKS, but the story has a semi-happy ending. After years of delays, the hotel was found liable for discrimination against Native people and forced to pay tens of thousands of dollars in damages in late 2025. Though this hotel is not the government, I think it's a good example of the racism Native people still face in our own territories.

2024: Brat Summer swept the nation the same year President Biden formally (and finally) apologized for the century-long atrocity of government-operated Indian Boarding Schools.

2025: Everyone in the world bought a Labubu the same year Leonard Peltier was released from prison. Around fifty years after his sentencing, and after decades of pressure from activists and politicians, President Biden commuted Peltier's two life sentences, allowing him to spend his later years at home with his community. Even after decades in prison, he's still participating in marches and fighting for the rights of Native people at every turn.

2026: This book came out, and you're reading it right now. Other stuff probably happened afterward, but I don't have a crystal ball. Sorry!

2021 — 2022 — 2024 — 2025 — 2026

EXTRA EXTRA, READ ALL ABOUT IT!

Natives have present problems too!

When media outlets talk about Native people and Native issues, we're often presented as a past tense problem and "relics of history." The attitude is that since we "no longer exist," you don't have to think about us unless it's Thanksgiving or the Kansas City Chiefs are in the Super Bowl.

The thing about that is, it sweeps under the rug all of the issues Natives are dealing with now! If we only exist in the past, there's no reasons for people to invest, financially or politically, in helping any of the ten million Native people in this country today.
The first step to a solution is awareness, so here are a few issues currently plaguing Indian Country.

→ One-third of homes on Navajo Nation land don't have running water! Over one hundred thousand people live on the Navajo Reservation of Arizona, New Mexico, and Utah. That means tens of thousands of people have to travel, in some cases fifty miles both ways daily, to get enough water to survive. So far, the government has refused to build infrastructure to give Navajo Nation citizens the running water they desperately need.

→ Because many reservations are in rural areas, many Native people live in "food deserts," far from any grocery stores or with limited access to healthy foods. This has caused food insecurity in tribal communities. Additionally, since most of the food a lot of Native folks have access to is heavily processed, it's caused diabetes, high blood pressure, and other health ailments to spike in our communities.

→ Though recent federal legislation like Savanna's Act and the Not Invisible Act have helped address the Missing and Murdered Indigenous Women and Missing and Murdered Indigenous People epidemics, the issue is by no means solved. More of our brothers and sisters are stolen from our communities every day, and increased awareness and government support would really help.

→ Native people die by suicide at significantly higher rates than any other ethnic group. Most heartbreaking are the suicide rates of our Native youth, which are nearly three times the national average. There are so many reasons for this, such as systemic poverty in tribal communities and IHS clinics rarely having enough resources to address mental health issues. There's a ton of research showing that Native sports mascots and Native stereotypes are directly harmful to Native kids' self-esteem. When a Native youth only sees people like them portrayed as red-faced savages or "ancient history," it's not going to give them hope for their present or there even being a future with them in it. If you're a Native kid reading this, take it from me, the author of this book who was once a Native youth: You have a future.

→ We also face police brutality at significantly higher rates than most other ethnic groups. Native people are killed by police at over three times the rate of white folks.

→ Poverty is common in tribal communities, with over a quarter of Native folks in America living below the poverty line. This is higher than any other ethnic group and more than double the national average. The Pine Ridge Indian Reservation, one of the largest Indian reservations in the country, is often cited as one of the poorest places in America, with the median per capita income in some areas being as low as $8,768 per year.

Though Natives got the right to vote decades ago, voter suppression in tribal communities is commonplace. Most reservations are in rural areas, and some Native folks have to drive as far as 150 miles to cast a ballot. In some states, Native voter turnout has the potential to flip elections, so it's hard not to view this Native voter suppression as being at least partially on purpose.

Cultural and language preservation is a big issue in tribal communities. Many of our culture and language experts are elders who won't be around forever. Though it's a constant struggle to pass our traditions down to the next generation, something that's helped are grants and tribal business profits giving tribes the resources to fund cultural and language programs. For example, my tribe recently released the Cowlitz Salish Dictionary as a smartphone app for tribal members, using technology to preserve our language in a real way.

Though Native people have had huge legal wins when it comes to tribal sovereignty, maintaining that sovereignty and pushing the federal government to honor their treaty obligations is a constant legal fight that won't be ending any time soon.

A lot of people don't know about these issues. My hope is that by making you aware of this stuff, you'll think about it the next time you're at the polls. When deciding who to vote for in your next local, state, or national election, don't be afraid to ask candidates what their plans are for Indian Country and if any of these issues are at the top of their minds (and they really should be because, I mean, seriously).

INDIGENOUS FOLKS AROUND THE WORLD DON'T HAVE IT MUCH EASIER

This book is USA-focused because that's what I know best, but there are around 476 million Indigenous people around the world. All Indigenous groups have our own struggles caused by colonization. How I tend to think about it is, no two tribes were screwed the same way by all of this stuff, but we all got screwed just the same.

In total, there are around five thousand Indigenous tribes around the world within the borders of ninety different countries. The United States is a big part of that puzzle, but tribes outside of the United States have their own unique challenges. Here are a handful of (countless!) examples.

The First Nations people of **Canada** were victims of what's called the "Sixties Scoop," where it became a Canadian governmental policy to send social workers to Indigenous peoples' homes to "scoop up" First Nations kids. These kids were forcibly removed from their birth families and sent to foster homes so they could be adopted by white families. The First Nations families had no say in this practice, and it was common from the 1960s until as late as the 1980s. The effects of the Sixties Scoop are still felt within Canada's First Nations communities.

The Māori people of **New Zealand** often have to pressure the New Zealand government to honor their treaty obligations. As recently as 2024, the New Zealand Parliament attempted to pass a bill reinterpreting their treaty with the Māori people that would have weakened Māori sovereignty. Nearly one hundred thousand people attended in-person protests against this bill, and it was THANKFULLY voted down due to public outcry.

The hundreds of Indigenous tribes of **Australia** are some of the oldest cultures in the world, and yet they are the only First Nations peoples in the British Commonwealth that do not have a treaty in place. A vote even came before the country to add its Indigenous people to Australia's constitution as recently as 2023, but it was voted down. The work continues, and I hope the Indigenous peoples of Australia receive recognition soon.

The Sámi people of **Norway** face constant struggles of racism, stolen land, food sovereignty, loss of fishing, hunting, and herding rights, and the warming Arctic threatening their traditional way of life.

The Ainu and Ryūkyūans people of **Japan** are constantly pushing back against the destruction of their cultures through forced assimilation and the Japanese and American governments stealing their lands for the purposes of building military bases.

The several dozen Indigenous tribes of **Russia** receive next to no representation in Russian politics, and what little rights and protections they do have are rarely enforced. Many of the Indigenous tribes of Russia, including the Tuvans and Yakuts, are not officially recognized by the Russian government.

American nuclear tests on the **Bikini Atoll** have left the homeland of many Marshallese poisoned by radioactive fallout, causing massive health complications in the Marshallese people. The Bikini Atoll is so uninhabitable that most Marshallese have had to flee the island. Today, a half dozen or so people remain on the atoll.

The Amazigh people of **Morocco and Algeria** face constant struggles like forced assimilation, stolen land, and the arrest of vocal Amazigh activists. The government of Morocco gives the Amazigh little assistance and constantly drags its feet to aid Amazigh people affected by natural disasters like the 2023 Al Haouz earthquake. The government didn't even recognize the Amazigh until 2011!

The Ogoni people of **Nigeria** are in the middle of a decades-long fight against the Shell Oil Company. Shell's oil drilling caused severe damage to the Ogoni homelands, bringing poverty, lack of clean water, and severe health issues to the Ogoni. Instead of siding with the Ogoni, the country of Nigeria executed activists fighting for the rights of the Ogoni people.

The Maasai people of **Tanzania** have faced forced relocation from their homelands by the Tanzanian government as recently as the 2020s to make room for infrastructure projects and tourism. Though the Tanzanian government claims the recent land evictions of seventy thousand Maasai are voluntary, the facts and boots-on-the-ground experiences of the Maasai disagree. The United Nations even stepped in, siding with the Masaai and demanding Tanzania stop this practice.

The San and Khoekhoe people of **South Africa** faced over a century of oppression from the effects of European colonization, including forced labor and attempted genocide. The Native Lands Act of 1913 prevented Indigenous peoples of South Africa from owning land in their own territories. The San and Khoekhoe people still feel the economic and cultural effects of these and other anti-Indigenous practices to this day.

The Yanomami people of Brazil and Venezuela are in a constant battle with illegal gold miners, who brought diseases, poisoned the Yanomami homelands, and led to the deaths of many South American Indigenous people. Tens of thousands of miners operated largely unchecked, stealing the resources of the Yanomami people until the Brazilian government finally intervened in 2023.

Many of the Indigenous tribes of **South America**, including the Asháninka peoples, are fighting illegal mining operations as well as the deforestation of the Amazon rainforest poisoning their homelands. Industrial soy and sugarcane farming has pushed many tribes like the Guarani peoples off of their traditional lands.

The examples in this chapter barely scratch the surface of this stuff and are not meant to be a complete list. If you're Indigenous and you want to include the ways colonization screwed over you and your people, please add them in the blank spot below!

Want your own tribe in this book? Write all the terrible things colonizers did or are doing to you and your people here. Let's shame them together!

THESE PEOPLE AREN'T INVITED TO THE POWWOW

(unabridged)

If you've gotten this far, you know that Columbus, Andrew Jackson, the Pope, and John Wayne aren't invited to the powwow, but if you were looking for more people to disinvite to your next big Native gathering, here are a couple more people to add to that list!

RICHARD HENRY PRATT: He coined the phrase, "Kill the Indian, save the man," so I'm here to tell him to "kill your appetite, save your money," because you are not buying any Indian tacos at the powwow!

JAMES CAMERON: He famously stole the story of the Lakota people and used it in his weird blue alien *Avatar* series, and now he'll never eat a delicious blue corn muffin, because he is not invited to the powwow!

CALVIN COOLIDGE: While president of the United States in the 1920s, Calvin Coolidge blocked my tribe's federal recognition, and we had to wait another eighty years to get federally recognized. That pales in comparison to the infinity years he's gonna have to wait to watch a professional-level shawl dance, because he is not invited to the powwow!

JOHNNY DEPP: He dressed in redface to play the role of Tonto in the 2013 *The Lone Ranger* film. Now the Lone Ranger isn't the only person who's going to be "lone." It's also going to be Johnny Depp, because he's not invited to the powwow!

ANN COULTER: In 2025, political commentator Ann Coulter said, "We didn't kill enough Indians," after watching a speech from Diné scholar Melanie Yazzie. If Coulter says anything else about Natives, we're not going to hear it, because we'll be at the powwow and she isn't invited.

DONALD TRUMP: He popularized using the name Pocahontas as a slur, and that's so messed up. Seriously, dude. What the hell. Clearly, he's not invited to the powwow.

WSU FRESHMAN: When I was a student at Washington State University, a freshman found out I was Native and kept asking me questions like, "If tribes are their own sovereign nations, why do Indians get to vote in United States elections?" He was accusatory and weird about it, but now I get to be the accusatory one because I'm accusing him of not being invited to the powwow!

KRISTI NOEM: As the former governor of South Dakota, Kristi Noem was notoriously awful to Natives living in her state. It got so intense that many tribes banned her from visiting any of their reservations. There's another place she's banned, and that's right, it's the powwow! And for running the Department of Homeland Security, where she detained, deported, and displaced many Indigenous people seeking asylum, some of whom are literally indigenous to the United States, she's also banned from any and all beading circles. May her shame be carried on every one of her sloppy beadwork stitches.

L. FRANK BAUM: He wrote the *Wizard of Oz* series of books in the early 1900s and also wrote a series of essays advocating for the extermination of all Native people. Now I'm advocating for the extermination of his name from any powwow invite lists. Sorry, not sorry!

UNIVERSITIES: Many colleges have the bones of thousands of Native people storied in their archives and are refusing to return them to their rightful communities. If you're in a decision-making position at these schools and aren't working to repatriate these remains, then I'm repatriating your name right off the powwow invite list. Looking at you, Harvard; University of California, Berkeley; and Indiana University!

JOHN GAST: In 1872, he painted *American Progress*, the work of art most associated with the term "Manifest Destiny." Back in the 1800s, Manifest Destiny was coined as a government-approved tagline claiming that it was America's god-given right to colonize the continent. For helping popularize this gross belief, it's my creator-given right to tell John Gast to Manifest his ass away from this powwow because he's not invited!

HIGH SCHOOL PRINCIPALS: Every year, Native students decorate their high school graduation caps with regalia and eagle feathers to include their cultures in this life accomplishment. In some cases, schools will use arbitrary rules to single out Native kids, ordering them to remove and destroy their regalia. If they refuse, they're not allowed to receive their diploma with their class. A lot of Native youths don't have an easy path to their education, and this can be so traumatizing. I want these kids to know they should be proud of their cultures, and they can absolutely wear their regalia at the powwow, which these principals are NOT invited to.

ABE LINCOLN: He ordered the execution of thirty-eight members of the Dakota tribe in 1862 in what is the largest mass execution in United States history. It's one of many dark moments in our country's complicated past and not discussed enough when talking about Lincoln's legacy. Also, his big hat is stupid. Not invited to the powwow!

ORGANIZATIONS: Any organization that only engages with Native people for Native American Heritage Month in November and forgets about us for the rest of the year, well I'm forgetting about you when I'm putting my powwow invite list together!

SAMMY FAIN and **SAMMY CAHN:** They wrote the racist song from the *Peter Pan* soundtrack called "What Made the Red Man Red?" and now I guess they'll never know the answer to that question because they're not invited to the powwow!

PRETENDIANS: Anyone who knowingly lies about being Native to get jobs and opportunities set aside for Native people are for sure not invited to the powwow. It's about time they faced a few consequences!

TOMAHAWK CHOP: Anyone who does the tomahawk chop at sporting events and then when Natives say they're not comfortable with it, dig in their heels and say, "We're honoring you," well now they can tomahawk chop away from the powwow that they're not invited to!

ICE AGENTS: No one is illegal on stolen land, and ICE agents aren't legal at the powwow because they're not invited.

GUTZON BORGLUM: This artist is responsible for Mount Rushmore, which defaced the Lakota people's sacred site in the Black Hills with the faces of several Founding Fathers. You know whose face you're not going to see at the powwow? Gutzon Borglum. In your face!

Also, I visited Mount Rushmore recently, and I couldn't help but take this picture.

A VISUAL REPRESENTATION OF HOW A LOT OF NATIVE PEOPLE FEEL ABOUT MOUNT RUSHMORE

Not sure what you were expecting here. And for the record, it looks dumb and ugly in person.

IN CONCLUSION

“Indian 101” or “Native 101” is a term Native folks throw around when describing interactions with non-Natives. It’s a shorthand way to describe the moment when you, usually out of nowhere, have to summarize hundreds of years of Native identities, histories, and cultures to someone before you can have the conversation you want to have. It’s a lot!

As a TV writer, most of my Indian 101 conversations are about jokes. Pitching a joke about frybread to a TV show writer’s room goes way slower when you have to explain to the room not only what frybread is but also how frybread was a food created out of necessity and trauma. After the United States government forced Native people onto reservations, flour and salt (ingredients used to make frybread) were all the military left behind for Native folks to eat. That puffy, deeply unhealthy (and yet deeply delicious) treat is how they made do.

Explaining that stuff doesn’t just slow down the conversation and make the joke-writing process a lot harder. It’s also exhausting! Oftentimes, non-Natives have next to no baseline knowledge when it comes to anything to do with Indian Country. I write jokes for a living, but imagine this in more important settings, like a politician trying to pass laws to stop the Missing and Murdered Indigenous Women epidemic, or a tribe defending their treaty rights to prevent a local government from building on their land, or a Native adult using their tribal ID as identification to enter a bar to hang out with their friends. It’s tough when the bouncer has never seen a tribal ID card before and was trained to treat everything they don’t recognize as a fake ID, which a tribal card very much isn’t.

If, when trying to tackle nuanced and important issues, you're constantly having to stop to explain the super basics, it gunks up the works faster than a car engine full of ice cream.

I love talking about my culture. The first time I had an Indian 101 conversation in college, I was so happy to educate that person! Imagine how I felt after the thousandth time. At a certain point, it becomes a job you're not paid for, and it feels like you're being treated more as an information source than a human being, which sucks.

My goal in writing this book was to give everyone some baseline knowledge to hopefully prevent some of these Indian 101 conversations. Also to convince you to show up to powwows and start handing out trophies, but that's beside the point.

For Natives, I hope reading this book gave you some laughs, some catharsis, and an easy resource the next time a coworker, friend, classmate, or random person on the internet asks you a weird question about Native stuff. Oh, and sorry I talked about my tribe's casino so much. I'm proud is all. I'm sure your tribe has cool stuff too!

For non-Natives, I hope this book equipped you with basic knowledge about Indian Country. Keep in mind that I'm just one person with my own opinions. Some Natives agree with me, some don't, and that's fine. If I can help prevent some weird conversations, I'll consider it a win. This book shouldn't be the end of your Native education journey but the beginning, so don't forget to seek out other points of view. The last several pages of this book are my personal recommendations of awesome Native things, people, and organizations you should check out, so you don't have any excuse!

Lastly, I hope this book made you laugh a bunch! I also hope it helped you appreciate the beautiful Indigenous cultures and people in the world with, like, a 50% less chance of you putting your foot in your mouth while doing it. You're still going to mess up, I'm sure.
I mess up too! Screwing up is what being human is all about!

The key is to be respectful, acknowledge your screwups, don't dig in your heels when you're wrong, understand you're a guest in someone else's culture, and try not to get your dirty footprints everywhere.

Now, there's one more extremely important part of this first stop in your Native listening and learning journey.

You've got to sign your diploma!

Turn the page!

INDIAN 101 GRADUATE

DIPLOMA

SUCCEED

This diploma proves that the undersigned has a baselevel understanding of Native issues. They promise not to call work meetings powwows or use the term "Indian giver," they will let any elder cut in front of them in line at a buffet, they will not mess up any land acknowledgments, they will watch all of the films of Wes Studi, they will think of Native people every month and not only in November, if they ever see a post about Land Back on social media they'll mutter to themselves "hell yeah," and if they ever meet *Twilight* author Stephenie Meyer, they'll try not to get bit by her so they don't get infected by her (alleged, ayy) werewolf curse.

YOUR NAME HERE
Not a total shitass

Joey Clift

JOEY CLIFT (Cowlitz)
Indian Guide, but like, the non-spiritual kind

It's not a hand turkey, but I mean, come on. What is?

ACKNOWLEDGMENTS

These people ARE invited to the powwow!

I grew up on the Tulalip rez in a low-income household and never thought I could have the life and career that I have. Being able to write this book, which you went out of your way to find and used your precious time to read, has been such a wonderful and humbling experience. I have a laundry list of people to thank for helping me make it happen.

I owe my mom, my grandmother, and all my ancestors for keeping the Cowlitz fire burning for me. Their passion for our people and desire to continue our culture has allowed me to help carry the torch for our current generation of Cowlitz relatives. Also, I just really appreciate my mom for being a weirdo artist and all-around badass Indian who helped raise me and encouraged me to become the weirdo comedy writer that I am today. Love you, Mom! Sorry I don't call more!

To my dad, a career freelance carpenter who hustled every day of his life: He was the hardest-working person I have ever met, and I owe him immensely for instilling in me a solid work ethic. Even if he didn't understand all of my weird comedy bits, and I'm not sure if he totally got what I do for a living, he never stopped encouraging me to follow my dreams, and I wouldn't have the life I have if he hadn't believed in me. Thank you, Dad. I miss you and am so proud I got to be your son.

To my Cowlitz ancestors, thank you for fighting since the 1850s for our tribe's culture and federal recognition so that today, nearly two hundred years later, our tribe can prosper. Through them, I understand deeply the Indigenous mentality that it's important to plant trees so your children's children can enjoy shade.

To our Cowlitz culture and language experts, tribal and general council members, cousins, youth, lost birds, crotchety elders, and messy aunties and uncles: We might argue here and there, but I'm grateful that all of us are working together in our own ways to push our people forward.

To my girlfriend, Goldie Chan, for encouraging me to write this book, for smiling politely every time I show you a picture of an orange cat that looks kind of like Garfield, and for still being impressed whenever I take you to Ilani and show you that my tribal ID gets me a discount at the restaurants. Thank you, and I love you. Great relationship. No notes!

To my editor, Amanda Meadows, and the fantastic folks at Andrews McMeel Publishing! Around ten years ago, when I was a baby sketch comedy writer tackling important comedic subjects like, "What if Spider-Man could rap?" Amanda was one of the first people who encouraged me to use comedy to explore my Native identity. She even edited my Native comedy zine, *The American Indian Ready to Wear Catalog 2018*! She not only helped me develop this book, she also helped cultivate a comedic POV that's shaped a sizeable chunk of the past decade of my life. Thanks, Amanda!

My digital series *Gone Native* and my first short film, *Telling People You're Native American When You're Not Native Is a Lot Like Telling a Bear You're a Bear When You're Not a Bear,* helped me figure out the right tone to use when tackling Native issues through a comedic lens. I can't thank David Kantrowitz, Jason Grasl, Alec Sherrie, the Yes, And . . . Laugher Lab, Caty Borum, Bethany Hall, Mik Moore, Crystal Echohawk and IllumiNative, Erika Soto Lamb at Paramount, Jesse Goldman at Loose World, Harold Moss at FlickerLab, Pop Culture Collab, and my executives at Comedy Central and Dropout enough for helping me prove that there's an audience for jokes about Native stuff!

While I was a mentor for the Native Student Center at WSU, I spent much of that time feeling that I wasn't "Native enough." I owe a true debt to Director of Native American Programs Barbara Aston for taking the time to mentor me and for telling me that culture isn't a contest, that it's okay to not be an expert on the traditions of your people, that we all contribute to our tribes in different ways, and that all our ancestors want is for us to be happy. Whenever I struggle with my place in Indian Country, I think back on our conversations and smile. Go Cougs!

To the group chats, thanks for being a place to talk at length about professional wrestling, Native stuff, politics, hamburgers, high school, comedy scene drama, petty complaints, and the weird issues of my neighborhood. May we continue to boost each other up and trash the haters for years to come.

To all the Native folks in my life, from longtime friends in my tribe and Native Hollywood to folks I've chatted with in passing. Wherever we are in our lives and journeys, we're unafraid to encourage each other and help each other process the weirdness that is being Native in the twenty-first century. Even if we're not from the same tribe, y'all are family.

To everyone I've had the joy of performing with, writing for, or cracking jokes with in a writer's room. From high school talent shows, to Cable 8, to sketch and improv shows at comedy theaters like the Upright Citizen's Brigade, The Pack, iO West, and Second City Hollywood, and any podcast that's given me even a second of airtime. I've been doing this for over half my life, and my favorite part about it is the collection of interesting chuckleheads I get to laugh with along the way.

To anyone who's ever gone to one of my shows, listened to one of my podcast interviews, read one of my articles, shared one of my comedy videos, or sent me kind words about any projects or shows I've worked on, truly, thank you. Y'all are the best!

To my manager, Chris Coggins; my lawyer, Matthew Wallerstein; and anyone who's ever hired me for a job, flown me out for a talk, or booked me on a show, thank you for the trust and support.

To my school and college teachers and respected elders—Terry Goedel, Al Fruetel, Richard Walsh, Tory Klementsen, Kevin Craft, Marvin Marcelo, Glenn Johnson, Richard Taflinger, Wayne Popeski, Kenji Kitatani, Mark Anderson, and Roberta Kelly—thanks for giving a weird kid who probably disrupted class a bit too much a push in the right direction.

To my comedy teachers and mentors—Henry Normal, Tim Kalpakis, Nick Wiger, Eric Moneypenny, Heather Anne Campbell, Sam Brown, Chris Nee, Scott Hallock, Travis Fields, Gabriel Garza, and Donick Cary—thanks for being encouraging and for humoring me when I asked way too many questions about comedy writing.

To Jonathan Joss and Charlie Hill, two Native comedic voices who helped pave the way, thanks for helping make the entertainment industry a little nicer for all the Natives coming up behind you. We owe you a debt!

To Karissa Valencia, my boss on *Spirit Rangers* and my friend in life, thanks for inviting me to work on such a special show and for helping me figure out how to handle the "representation sweats" without having a heart attack. May our *Spirit Rangers* writer's room group chat be forever active.

To my friends in the nonprofit space, thanks for doing the work, for showing me that comedy can be a tool for narrative change, for inviting me to all of your fun parties, and for not saying anything when I eat most of the cheese off of your well-stocked charcuterie boards.

To anyone who didn't believe in me, thanks for filling me with the most powerful motivator of all: spite!

To Mick Foley, Conan O'Brien, The Beastie Boys, Henry Winkler, Ed Solomon, Steve Pool, The Blue Scholars, Fiona Apple, Jim Davis, Gary Larson, Thomas Lennon, Hideo Kojima, and the teams behind *Final Fantasy VI*, *Chrono Trigger*, *Earthbound*, and *Fallout 2*. When I was a kid, I didn't know that I was allowed to tell stories for a living. Your creative works gave me the permission to dream.

And finally, to my tribe's many, many, many Facebook groups, thank you for mostly saying nice things about me. I'm doing my best!

GLOSSARY FOR THE ALLIES

Like any culture, Native folks have our own slang to describe things. Here are some words and definitions to help the non-Native allies at the powwow.

Auntie: A Native woman who is older than you. Usually a term of endearment and has almost nothing to do with actual blood relation.

Ayyy: Often said to punctuate a roast joke.

Braids: A traditional hairstyle a lot of Natives wear. Though this hairstyle originated in many Plains tribes, it's become kind of a pan-Indian thing that folks wear regardless of tribe.

Commodity Cheese: Also called "government cheese." A type of oily cheese that the government often distributes on reservations.

Commodity Butter: "Commodity cheese," but the butter version!

Commod Bod: The way your body looks after eating too much commodity cheese and commodity butter.

Cousin: A term of endearment from one Native to another Native or big-time ally. Rarely has anything to do with blood relation or if you're even from the same tribe. Sometimes shortened to "Cuz" or "Cuzzo."

Elder: An older member of a tribe. Treated with respect, honor, and always allowed to eat first at dinner.

Fancy Dance, Shawl Dance: Types of dances you'd see at a powwow. If you haven't seen these awe-inspiring dances in person, what the heck are you waiting for?

GWE: Short for General Welfare Exclusion. A type of payment tribes can make to members of that tribe to aid in general welfare, housing, food, and anything else as long as it's not too fancy. It's usually paid for out of grant funding or profits from tribally owned businesses. No matter how they got it, it's not free money. The tribe earned it fair and square!

HUD Housing: Short for Housing and Urban Development. This is a type of cheap housing built by the government and often seen on reservations. It ain't the Ritz!

Indian Country: A term used to loosely describe Native peoples as a population, or to refer to specific geographic regions particularly steeped in Native peoples and cultures.

Native Hollywood: Used to describe the few hundred or so Native folks who work in the entertainment industry. If you're reading this and you're a part of Native Hollywood, thanks for buying my book, cuz!

NDN: Said out loud, it sounds like "Indian." Not an acronym. It's kind of a shorthand folks use to write "Indian" while also looking rad.

Pan-Indian: Though all of our tribes are vastly different in terms of culture, some aspects of different tribal cultures have become part of Native monoculture, meaning we've all kind of adopted it over the years. Dreamcatchers, Indian tacos, beadwork, and that sort of thing are all considered by a lot of people to be "pan-Indian."

Per Cap: Short for "Per Capita." Since, technically, all tribally owned businesses are owned by all members of the tribe, this is a payment tribes make to their people to split those profits. It's kind of like a stock dividend. Only a small percentage of tribes are wealthy enough to distribute per caps to their members, so if you get 'em, lucky you! Still not free money though!

Pretendian: Someone who is lying about being Indian. Short for "pretend Indian." (Non-Natives, please don't say this too much.)

Regalia: The ornate outfits you see Native folks wear at powwows and other traditional events are broadly called "regalia." Pro tip: If you refer to it as a costume, it's super disrespectful and you may get punched in the face.

Rez: Short for "reservation."

Rez Dogs: Dogs who live on the reservation, don't have an owner, and the entire community takes care of. They're equal parts rugged and adorable.

Rezzy: A slang term for a Native who has that rez stank on 'em. Used as a term of endearment OR to slam someone, depending on the context. Generally, not a term non-Natives should use unless they want to get cussed out so loudly their ancestors will hear it.

Sacrit: A purposeful misspelling of the word "sacred" for folks who are particularly cool or rezzy.

Snag: Used as a verb, to hook up with someone romantically. Used as a noun, someone you are currently hooking up with. If you've been snagging, congrats!

'Skoden: Short for "let's go then." Often used when you'd like one or many people to go, then.

'Stoodis: Short for "let's do this." Often used when you'd like one or many people to do this. Regularly the last word said before a fistfight breaks out.

Tradish: Short for "traditional." Used by the most sacrit Natives.

Turtle Island: A common term Native folks use to refer to North America, because North America's outline kind of looks like an adorable turtle (awww).

Two-Spirit: A term to describe our Indigenous relatives who are not on the colonial spectrums of gender and/or sexuality. Generally used with respect and reverence. Two-Spirit is a new term (coined in 1990), so it's by no means traditional, but it's been adopted quickly within Indian Country. Pro tip: Though we love our non-Native trans and nonbinary allies, two-spirit is a term only used to describe Indigenous folks who fall on that spectrum. Try not to use those words interchangeably if you can help it.

Uncle: The male version of "Auntie"!

Wes: Short for legendary Cherokee actor and film producer Wes Studi. We say his name so much that it saves time to shorten it.

TONS OF NATIVE THINGS AND PEOPLE TO CHECK OUT THAT AREN'T THIS BOOK!

This book isn't the be-all end-all of Native knowledge. Native people aren't a monolith, and I'm only one dude and can't speak for everybody! Plus, the Native experience isn't all genocide and ragging on Columbus (though that is a BIG part of it). There are a ton of Native folks in the arts, fashion, comedy, politics, and many other places who are all doing great, Native-forward work.

If you want a well-rounded view of Indian Country, seek out as many Native perspectives as you can. Here are a few people, organizations, businesses, and things I think are worth exploring! If you're wondering if my tribe's casino Ilani is on this list, you're damn right it is.

There are a ton of **Native nonprofits** doing good work within Indian Country. **NDN Collective** is a leading voice in the #LandBack movement with education tools about all things Land Back. **Navajo Water Project** is working hard to bring water infrastructure to the Navajo Nation. **Protect the Sacred** is educating and empowering the next generation of Native leaders, the **National Native American Boarding School Healing Coalition** is doing fantastic work addressing the trauma caused by Indian boarding schools, the **Institute of American Indian Arts** is training the next generation of Native creatives, **Native Organizers Alliance** gives tools and assistance to Native grassroots organizers, and the **National Indigenous Women's Resource Center** is working to help end the Missing and Murdered Indigenous Women epidemic. If you want to help Native people, support these organizations with money!

Native people are hilarious, and there are a ton of **Native stand-up comedians** killing it in and out of Indian Country. I love **Zebadiah Nofire**, **Siena East**, **Jackie Keliiaa**, **Howie Echo-Hawk**, **Jim Ruel**, **Marc Yaffee**, **Joshua Emerson**, **Josh Fournier**, **Dakota Ray Hebert**, **Brian Bahe**, **Blake Pickens**, **Ernie Tsosie**, **Monique Moreau**, **and Jana Schmieding**. If you like the classics, check out **Charlie Hill**, and if you want to see some good live Native comedy, seek out the live-touring Native stand-up shows *Good Medicine*, *Bad Indian* and the *Native American Comedy Jam*.

If you're into **sketch comedy,** watch the **1491s'** YouTube back catalog! They were the first all-Native sketch comedy group to go viral back in 2009, and since then, they've become a force in comedy. Their members—**Sterlin Harjo**, **Ryan RedCorn**, **Bobby Wilson**, **Migizi Pensoneau**, and **Dallas Goldtooth**—are all worth following individually and collectively; they've also worked on a lot of great shows, like the hilarious stage play *Between Two Knees* and the hit series *Reservation Dogs*.

Speaking of *Reservation Dogs*, there are some great **Native-created TV shows** worth checking out! *Rutherford Falls*, cocreated by **Sierra Teller Ornelas**, and *Reservation Dogs,* cocreated by **Sterlin Harjo**, are the first two television shows in United States history created by Native people. *Spirit Rangers*, created by **Karissa Valencia**, is a fantastic Native-created kids' series, and *Dark Winds*, executive produced by and starring **Zahn McClarnon**, is a fun Native supernatural drama series. Shout-out to *Molly of Denali*. Though *Molly*'s "created by" credit does not belong to a Native person, they employed a ton of Natives and tackle all of their stories with authenticity and heart. If you've got little ones, *Molly of Denali* is definitely worth a watch. Full disclosure, I wrote on *Molly of Denali* and *Spirit Rangers*. If you liked this book, you'll love those shows!

For more Native-created content, **FNX - First Nations Experience** is a great broadcast channel with its own streaming app that'll give you easy access to a ton of great Native-made films and television shows for free!

Native podcasts are having a moment right now, with great options in every genre. If you like comedy, *Sage-Based Wisdom,* hosted by super funny comedians **Brian Bahe** and **Jana Schmieding,** is a hilarious listen. *All My Relations* is a fantastic dive into the modern Native experience. *This Land* is a great documentary podcast about the nuances of tribal sovereignty, and *Pretendians* explores ethnic fraud within Indian Country in a way that is easily digestible. *Reel Indigenous* is also a good listen, with the show's hosts covering all things Native film and television.

And there's so much great stuff happening in **Native film**! If you like dramas, you'll love **Erica Tremblay's** *Fancy Dance*, starring **Lily Gladstone,** and **Sydney Freeland's** *Rez Ball*, co-written by **Sterlin**

Harjo. *Frybread Face and Me,* directed by **Billy Luther,** and *Powwow Highway,* starring Native comedy legend **Gary Farmer,** are hilarious Native-made films. If you prefer science fiction, *Slash/Back, Blood Quantum*, and *Prey* are so good! *Prey* wasn't written or directed by a Native, but it was produced by Comanche/Blackfeet tribal member **Jhane Myers,** it stars **Amber Midthunder,** and it's authentic and fun as hell from top to bottom. I also recommend checking out the short films, *The Roof, Headdress, Long Line of Ladies, Tiger, Courage, Inkwo for When the Starving Return, Cleaning's a Cakewalk,* and *Legend of Fry-Roti: Rise of the Dough.*

If you're looking for **Native directors** to follow, **Sterlin Harjo, Billy Luther, Sydney Freeland, Tazbah Chavez** and **Erica Tremblay** are ones to watch out for. Sterlin has an extensive indie film résumé, taking top prizes at major film festivals before running his own hit television shows *Reservation Dogs* and *The Lowdown*. Billy Luther has been killing it in the indie film space for years before breaking out with his top-rated comedy, *Frybread Face and Me*. Erica Tremblay's first feature, *Fancy Dance,* shows that she's a directorial force to be reckoned with, Sydney Freeland, with her extensive experience in television and film, is one of the top directorial voices in Native cinema, and Tazbah Chavez is one of the most in demand directors in the half hour sitcom space.

If you prefer **documentaries,** *Sugarcane*, co-directed by **Julian Brave NoiseCat,** and *Remaining Native,* directed by **Paige Bethmann,** are two incredible docs about the effects of government-run Indian boarding schools. *Lakota Nation vs. United States,* co-directed by **Jesse Short Bull,** gives a great deep dive into Lakota people's legal fight over the Black Hills of South Dakota. Short Bull also co-directed the fantastic *Free Leonard Peltier* about Peltier's long legal battle and his history of Native activism. *Ceremony*, directed by **Banchi Hanuse**, is a beautiful documentary about the history of the Nuxalk people. It's taken top awards at a bunch of big film festivals and is very worth tracking down.

Native folks are making waves in live theater, and there are a ton of great **Native playwrights** to watch. **Larissa FastHorse's** *The Thanksgiving Play* is a super funny satire about our country's complicated feelings about Thanksgiving. **Vera Starbard** celebrates her Alaska Native heritage through plays like *A Tlingit Christmas Carol*. **Kelly Lynne D'Angelo's** *Starry* often receives press and critical acclaim, and **Azie Dungey** wrote the book for *The Preacher's Wife*, which broke box office records in theaters around the country. If you're near Los Angeles, I also recommend checking out any shows put on by the theater ensemble **Native Voices**.

If you prefer **kickass music**, First Nations dubstep group **The Halluci Nation**, lo-fi hip hop artist **Mato Wayuhi**, rap group **Snotty Nose Rez Kids**, and solo rappers **Mic Jordan** and **Travis Thompson** are super cool. If indie rock is your thing, you'll love **Raye Zaragoza** and **Black Belt Eagle Scout**. If you prefer punk, **1876** and **Dead Pioneers** are great to thrash to. Special shout out to **Romeo Void**, a great new wave band that topped the charts in the 1970s and 1980s. The lead singer of Romeo Void is **Debora Iyall**, a member of the best tribe ever (Cowlitz! ayyy).

We've seen an explosion of contemporary **Native fashion** over the past few years! For a long time, the only fashion you ever saw Native people wear on camera were old dusty loincloths. It's empowering to see the younger generation take ownership over what "dressing Native" looks like. There are stylish streetwear brands like **The NTVS** and **Urban Native Era**; high fashion designers like **Bethany Yellowtail**, **Naiomi Glasses**, **House of Sutai**, and **Sky-Eagle Collection**; superstar Native fashion models like **Quannah Chasinghorse**; traditional beadwork artists like **Heather Stewart** releasing amazing work through timed "beadwork drops"; and Native fashion events like **Indigenous New**

York Fashion Week and the **Indigenous Fashion Gala** co-chaired by Taboo from the Black Eyed Peas! If you want the latest in Native fashion, jewelry, and accessories mainlined into your veins, every August, **Santa Fe Indian Market** in Santa Fe, New Mexico, is THE place for all things Native art and fashion.

And because this question comes up a lot, non-Natives can and should absolutely wear fashion from Native designers! Seriously, please buy their stuff! Not only would you be a good ally for supporting Native businesses you'll also get compliments because this stuff is beautiful!

We've also seen an explosion of **Native-run community spaces** in big cities, run by hip, young, Native creatives building places for contemporary Indigenous cultures to shine. **The Chapter House** is a great nonprofit putting on Native concerts, comedy shows, drag shows, workshops, and other events all over Los Angeles. On the East Coast, **Relative Arts NYC** is a neat Native-run consignment shop and art space that's become a centerpiece for Native art and culture in Manhattan, and **First Nations Performing Arts** is uplifting great Native productions in the city. **Tidelands,** in Seattle, and **Urban Native Collective,** in Cincinnati, are art-focused community spaces for Natives and Non-Natives to gather.

Native creatives are at the cutting edge of **visual arts,** with our work hanging in galleries globally! **Steven Paul Judd**, **Douglas Miles**, **Gregg Deal, Nicholas Galanin** and **Wendy Red Star** are doing amazing work in the pop art space, reimagining popular images and aesthetics through an Indigenous lens. **Jamie Okuma**, **Jeffrey Gibson**, and **Emma Robbins** combine Native artforms like beadwork and quillwork with contemporary aesthetics to create pieces that feel modern and traditional, and **Nonamey**'s rad cardboard sculptures are showing in galleries across the country!

In **animation**, **Quinne Larsen**, **Marie Bower**, **Nicolette Ray**, **Morgan Thompson**, **Amanda Strong**, **Joshua Herron**, and **Joseph Erb** are creating amazing animated works that tell contemporary Native stories through cartoons.

In **comics**, **Ricardo Caté's** *Without Reservations* is as funny, dark, and Native as it gets, and **Jakeli Swimmer's** *Around the Boundary Ink.* tackles nuanced Native issues through humor. **Arigon Starr's** *Super Indian* and **Jon Proudstar's** *Tribal Force* are great takes on the superhero genre with Native people front and center. **Julie Fiveash** is a super funny zine maker and cartoonist who I'm such a fan of that I had them illustrate this book! (Thanks, Julie!) I also strongly recommend checking out the work of **Jeffrey Veregge.** He was at the cutting edge of using Coastal Salish aesthetics in modern art, and he was regularly featured everywhere from the pages of Marvel Comics to the Smithsonian. He was so ahead of his time that the rest of the comics industry is still catching up.

If you're looking for in-person **Native comics events** to support, **IndigiPopX** is a great traveling Indigenous-focused pop culture convention with events all over the country!

As a **pro wrestling** dork, I've got to shout out **Gerald Brisco**, **Nyla Rose**, **KJ Orso**, **Karl Fredericks**, and **Sage Morin**. Other **Native athletes** to cheer for are NBA players **Kyrie Irving** and **Lindy Waters III**, NFL player **Creed Humphrey,** and runners **Rosalie Fish** and **Ku Stevens**. Also, the Haudenosaunee invented the sport of lacrosse, and the **Haudenosaunee Nationals** lacrosse team are some of the best players in the world!

In **books**, **Stephen Graham Jones** is one of the most respected authors in horror with *The Only Good Indians* being one (of many) of his books worth checking out. **Shane Hawk** and **Theodore**

C. Van Alst Jr.'s *Never Whistle at Night* is a fantastic Indigenous Horror anthology flying off store shelves as I write this. If you're into nonfiction books, **Matika Wilbur's** *Project 562*, **Anton Treuer's** *Everything You Wanted to Know about Indians But Were Afraid to Ask*, **Rebecca Nagle's** *By the Fire We Carry*, **Robin Wall Kimmerer's** *Braiding Sweetgrass*, **Kyle T. Mayes'** *An Afro-Indigenous History of the United States*, and **Elissa Washuta's** *White Magic* are great reads. Elissa Washuta is my actual cousin, but I'd recommend her book even if we weren't related!

In **literary fiction**, **Tommy Orange's** *There There*, **N. Scott Momaday's** *House Made of Dawn*, and **Louise Erdrich's** *Love Medicine* are incredible, and in the poetry space, I can't recommend enough the works of **Joy Harjo**, **Tommy Pico**, **Tazbah Chavez**, and **Kinsale Drake**. Kinsale also founded **NDN Girls Book Club**, a fantastic nonprofit dedicated to giving Native people a love for books and all things literature. If you've got a few extra bucks, definitely give them a donation!

In the **journalism** space, the most respected outlet in Native news is **ICT** (formally Indian Country Today), but there are additional outlets covering specific regions, like **Underscore Native News** in the Pacific Northwest. Some of the larger tribes even have their own news outlets (shoutout to **Navajo Times**!). For entertainment and pop culture coverage, **Native Max**, **indigenous.tv**, **Vincent Schilling, Laura Clark**, and **Red Pop! News** are great follows. A few other Native journalists you should keep on your radar are **Michelle Valles** at NBC4 in Los Angeles, **Alyssa London** formerly with MSNBC, **Jourdan Bennett-Begaye** with ICT, and **Sequoia Carrillo** with NPR.

There are a ton of rising Native stars in **local and national politics** doing great work in and out of Indian Country. Former Secretary of the

Interior **Deb Haaland**, Congresswoman **Sharice Davids**, Lieutenant Governor of Minnesota **Peggy Flanagan**, and former President of the Navajo Nation **Jonathan Nez** are all worth keeping an eye on. If you want to feel inspired, read up on **Wilma Mankiller.** She was the first woman elected as Principal Chief of the Cherokee Nation and is, as of 2022, the first Native woman featured on an official United States quarter. A historic politician, activist, and Indian Country badass if there ever was one.

Native influencers are killing it across social media. I recommend following **James Jones** (@NotoriousCree), **Tia Wood** (@tiamiscihk), **Che Jim** (@che_jim), **Michelle Chubb** (@indigenous_baddie), **Lucas Brown Eyes** (@lucasbrowneyes), **Shannon Baker** (@ shannonbaker), **Shauna Baker** (@shaunabaker), **Clark Feldman** (@ RefereeClark), and **Indigenous House** (@indigenoushouse) to add some NDN culture and humor to your timeline.

A common question on social media is, "Are there any **Native American restaurants**?" There are, and they rock. Some of my faves are the **Off the Rez** food truck and café in Seattle, the James Beard Award-winning **Fry Bread House** in Phoenix, **Big Bats** in Pine Ridge and the ultra-delicious **Tocabe** in Denver. On the fine dining side of things, "The Sioux Chef" **Sean Sherman** and "Chef Pyet" **Pyet DeSpain** are more than worth your time to track down.

Native culture is often crammed into the back of creaky museums, which is weird for sure. If you want to check out places that are doing thoughtful, curated exhibits about all things Native, I recommend the **Heard Museum** in Phoenix, **Dickinson College** in Carlisle, Pennsylvania, the **Autry Museum of the American West** in Los Angeles, the **Indian Pueblo Cultural Center** in Albuquerque, New Mexico, the **National Museum of the American Indian** in

Washington, DC, and the **Crazy Horse Memorial** in the Black Hills, South Dakota.

If you want to experience traditional and authentic Native cultures, go to a powwow! There are over a thousand powwows annually all across the United States and Canada. The website **powwows.com** is a great resource for powwows in your area, and they even have a "powwow etiquette guide" to tell you how to show up respectfully.

The Cowlitz powwow is every fall in southern Washington state, and it's a lot of fun. As I was writing this book, I had a chance to visit the Black Hills powwow in South Dakota, and it was crazy! There were over a thousand dancers on the floor at one time, and Leonard Peltier and Macklemore were there too! (Macklemore isn't Native, but he's a big-time ally/certified cuzzo.) Show up in time for "grand entry," which is the official start of powwow activities. Dances are a big part of powwows, and my favorites are the hoop dancers, but it's all amazing and something you should experience at least once in your life!

And finally, go to my tribe's casino, **Ilani,** in Ridgefield, Washington! Stay in the hotel and eat at one of our many restaurants! If there's one thing I want you to take away from this book, it's that Native people are still here and we rock. If there are TWO things I want you to take away from this book, it's that the Cowlitz casino resort Ilani is a short, scenic, twenty-minute drive from Portland, Oregon, and it's a fun time for everyone!

Anyone I missed? Reach out and I'll try to include them in a future printing!